Myf Porter's
GUIDE TO
Selling Property

"An absolute must read before selling your home." - Brian White

Published by:

Bas Publishing
ABN 30 106 181 542
F16/171 Collins Street
Melbourne Vic. 3000
Tel: (03) 9650 3200
Fax: (03) 9650 5077
Web: www.baspublishing.com.au
Email: mail@baspublishing.com.au

Copyright © 2004 Myf Porter

All rights reserved. This publication is copyright and may not be resold or reproduced in any manner (except excerpts thereof for bona fide study purposes in accordance with the Copyright Act) without the prior consent of the Publisher.

Every effort has been made to ensure that this book is free from error or omissions. However, the Publisher, the Authors, the Editor, or their respective employees or agents, shall not accept responsibility for injury, loss or damage occasioned to any person acting or refraining from action as a result of material in this book whether or not such injury, loss or damage is in any way due to any negligent act or omission, breach of duty or default on the part of the Publisher, the Authors, the Editor, or their respective employees or agents.

The National Library of Australia
Cataloguing-in-Publication entry:

Porter, Myf.
   Myf Porter's guide to selling property.

ISBN 1 920910 35 2.

   1. House selling - Australia - Handbooks, manuals, etc.
   2. House selling - New Zealand - Handbooks, manuals, etc.
   3. House selling - Australia - Case studies. I. Title.

333.3383

Page Layout and Design: Ben Graham

Printed in Australia by Shannon Books.

Contents

Foreword by Brian White	v
Introduction	vi
My Story	1
"Black and White is Never Right"	7
Emotion! Emotion!	11
Let's Help You to Choose...	17
Selling Methods Explained	41
WHO? Which Agent Will Best Suit Me?	65
Which Agency?	75
You Will Have to Sign Something!	79
Now Your Property is On the Market, What is Likely to Happen?	83
You Never Get a Second Chance...	93
If You are Going to Have a Signboard...	101
To Open or Not To Open	107
The Issue of Advertising?	119
Turning an Offer into a Sale!	135
Special Circumstances	147
So Great-Aunty Mary Has Left You Her House	149

The Chicken or the Egg	155
Sell or Rent and Retain	159
Extend or Buy	163
Renovate or Titivate? Or Nothing!	167
Divorce has Forced the Sale	171
Netting More Buyers	175
The Flexibility of Auctions	177
When/How do You Sell an Investment Property?	185
What Could Happen	191
Case Study 1 - Hugh and Samantha Thomas	193
Case Study 2 - Mary Gray	201
Case Study 3 - Bill and Joan Jones	207
Case Study 4 - Tom and Joanne Black	215
Case Study 5 - Agnes and Jack Smith	223
Case Study 6 - Norma and Roy Thomas	229
Conclusion	233
What Real Estate Agents Really Mean When They Say...	235

Foreword

Many times we are asked – how best to sell our property. This book fulfils that need. It will engender the confidence to enable you to sell your property in the way you believe to be best for you.

The beliefs in this book are Ray White beliefs. Its recommendations are our recommendations.

Myf is unique. She is able to express so eloquently the beliefs of Ray White. She created the training programmes that enabled Ray White to be relevant to the training needs of thousands of people who joined the industry during the past 20 years.

Now it is the turn for home owners across Australia and New Zealand to read her views on selling and how to select the strategy that best suits sellers.

BRIAN WHITE
Chairman Ray White Group

Introduction

I wanted to write this book because in all the years I've been coaching real estate salespeople, I have yet to find a book that is consistent with what I believe, or one that I could recommend either to sellers of property or to my students. I am concerned with some of the trends in real estate – trends that suggest there is only ONE way to sell real estate. My varied experience over many years has shown me that there is no one way that covers the selling of every home, in every area, in every situation. So, in this book I've endeavoured to express in everyday language what I have learnt and how that knowledge could simplify the selling of **your** home.

Before asking you to believe me, let me tell you my story.

My Story

Several years ago I took two of my grandchildren to Sovereign Hill at Ballarat where they were fascinated by the Apothecary (precursor to Pharmacist) who was actually making pills using two boards. How could I tell them that when I did my pharmacy apprenticeship with my father, I, too, made pills and performed those tasks that they associated with "the olden days"? How things change. One of my greatest beliefs is if we are not in a continual state of change, we will be left behind. It is so true that "when you're green you grow and when you're ripe you rot". Much of my life has been spent in a determination not to rot!

So I went from pharmacy to a wonderful marriage and four wonderful daughters. I then stayed home for some years and enjoyed the cooking, sewing and chauffeuring involved with four growing children. Then, for quite a few years, my husband Bruce and myself operated several large and very successful newsagencies in major shopping centres. Because of my love of books we developed a huge book section, and it was here that I had my first taste of the satisfaction of fitting client with requirement. The thrill of finding a book to suit a customer was nothing compared to the thrill of mixing buyer and house in my later career. Then, after 20 years of marital happiness, my husband became ill and it became necessary to sell our business. We then had two very precious years, just fishing, gardening and being together. It was not financially possible for us to exist any longer without any income so, of necessity, I became the breadwinner. Everyone expected me to go back to pharmacy but I'd always been fascinated by real estate. It was time to learn new skills and turn this interest into income.

That was when I had my first taste of the lack of respect afforded the real estate profession. I used to call selling the "oldest profession in the world" and claimed that I was proud to be a member of that profession, until one of my daughters told me what was usually considered the oldest profession! I've stopped using that phrase now. So many of my friends said "Real Estate?" with disbelief. It took me some months before I realised that I would be judged on how I worked in the industry and as long as I never did anything of which I could not be 100% proud, there wouldn't be a problem. I like to think that maxim contributed to my success in selling.

And I did have success, topping Queensland for Ray White in each year of my selling and being a partner in a very successful Ray White office. Then, my beloved Bruce passed away which, although expected, was devastating for the whole family. Brian White and Paul White decided that I should have a change.

This was in the very early '80s when training and real estate were not always words that were linked in one breath. We did have some training – which was more than most companies – but with about 40 company-owned offices and the move to franchising, formalised training programmes became a necessity. What a challenge at a time when I so badly needed one. Anyone who has suffered the loss of a beloved partner will know that you need work that will totally consume your every waking thought. Writing training and management programmes, deciding on content and duration of those programmes, and then implementing them sure does take up every waking moment – and lots of moments when other people sleep! What a learning experience! I also found that I loved the communication and the gathering and dispersing of that knowledge.

After several years we had a training programme referred to by people outside the company as the "very best available" – due in large part to the willingness of all our wonderful top salespeople and top managers/owners to share "what worked". My belief has always been that all our training must be SKILL-based. After several years, during which we had grown to more than 100 franchised offices in Queensland only, the decision was made to expand into New South Wales and Victoria. How fortunate I was to be given the opportunity to be in charge of this new Victorian operation and so began my love affair with Melbourne. I remember being asked to speak at a Real Estate of Victoria function on "Women in Real Estate" – women selling real estate were uncommon but a woman running a state company was unheard of! We started with nine offices in Victoria and in two years had a total of 33 offices. I learnt even more about selling, but this time, instead of selling "houses", I was selling the benefits of our support, training, network and name.

After several years in Melbourne, the training "bug" re-surfaced. By this time Ray White had expanded to about 300 offices throughout Queensland, NSW and Victoria and it was obvious that the training needed to be standardised and updated. So I became National Training Director, an awesome title that enabled me to live out of a suitcase for the majority of the time. One of our favourite family stories of this time was from my pre-school grandson who said that he had two grandmothers, "one lived in Toowoomba and the other lived on an aeroplane" – out of the mouths of babes!

With the acquisition of offices throughout New Zealand, I became almost an honorary Kiwi and with our move to Western Australia I had to learn that "coming from the east" was a burden I had to overcome. South Australia was, of course, a favourite destination –just a couple of hours from the Barossa Valley made sure that Adelaide had plenty of visits! So I learnt about real estate practices throughout Australia and New Zealand and I also found that the differences were quite superficial and mostly technical.

Now, Ray White has more than 600 offices throughout Australia, New Zealand, Papua New Guinea, Indonesia and Singapore. It is a fourth-generation, family-owned private company and the phenomenal success of this company is attributed to this unique combination.

There are so many real estate agents everywhere who are as passionate as I am about professionalism in real estate. All these

My Story

people have a total commitment to ethical practices and they choose to be in real estate because it is both exciting and rewarding.

When someone buys or sells a home, it is a totally emotional decision with almost no facts and figures to really assist with the decision. It is also one of the largest outlays a family makes. Someone once said buying and selling a house was the second most important decision that anyone made, with the first being who they should marry! With a decision as important as this, a decision usually based on emotion, there are bound to be some mistakes made. And someone must always be "blamed" for a mistake and there is just one group where the blame is placed – the real estate agent. It's like blaming the marriage celebrant if a marriage fails!

More than 20 years of practical hands-on experience in real estate, covering selling and managing, teaching and learning throughout Australia and New Zealand, have enabled me to crystalise what I believe really works and communicate that information to the sellers of personal real estate.

My wish is that by understanding the technicalities of the choices available to you, you will be able to positively participate in all the key decisions needed when selling.

"Black and White is Never Right"

The message of this book is: "Black and white is never right."

Out there somewhere is a person called "All". It's the person for whom those clothes with the tag "one size fits all" were made. I've yet to meet Mr or Mrs or Ms "All"! Actually, I've found that "one size fits all", fits very few. It's exactly the same in real estate. To say that one method of selling, WHATEVER that method may be, suits every person, every property and every area, just doesn't make sense. To say NEVER market with a price or to say that you must ALWAYS market with a price are the black and white answers. There are so many variables when it comes to selling that no one method is ever going to suit every person, situation and property. Different people, different circumstances, different properties all make for a potent mix!

The more experience I have accumulated, the more variances I have uncovered in the wonderful world of bringing residential sellers and buyers together. In recent years, particularly, I have seen many agents with almost religious zeal and fervour for only one idea and often their energy is mainly directed to negative recommendations – more "don'ts" than "do's". People who concentrate on negatives rarely put forth a positive recommendation or give you a choice of marketing methods. If an agent does not give you a choice, I would question their ability to understand "the big picture" of real estate.

In all my years of educating thousands of real estate salespeople, I have found no reason to wander from my most fundamental advice to all these salespeople, whether new to the industry or already experienced.

Be a good listener and give advice based on that person's needs, not on your own preconceived notions.

The decision to sell and then carrying that through will involve the whole family (and sometimes the extended family) in an emotional roller coaster ride. Thus, the reasoning behind efforts to standardise the selling process: "Let's analyse the process to the point where all property should be sold the same way. By taking away choices, we will make it more straightforward." Unfortunately, that theory does not work.

Black and white thoughts are required when devising a mathematical formula (sometimes!), but when it comes to dealing with the combinations of people and property there are so many shades of grey. Make sure that you find someone who will listen to you, make recommendations tailored to your specific needs and allow you to make a choice.

In summary:

- No two people, properties or situation are identical.
- Be cautious of agents who rely on negative suggestions.
- You should always be given a choice and that final choice is yours.
- Look for an agent who gives you advice based on YOUR needs.

Some estate agents think all homes are the same.

Ray White begs to differ.

Some estate agents will tell you all homes should be sold one way: their way.

They don't seem (or want) to understand, that private sales and auctions can both work equally well.

The way Ray White sees it, when you sell you home it should reflect your particular requirements.

At Ray White, we sell your home the way you want.

We will discuss the options with you and listen to your decision.

Ray White
REAL ESTATE

Emotion! Emotion!

Emotion rules when you sell. First of all comes the decision to sell. Options will have already been mentally explored.

I have discussed these options in a later part of the book. Think these issues through, as it's a lot of trouble to decide half way through the selling process that you don't really want to go through with it.

So why all this emotion?

What do sellers want? One thing that remains constant over all the years is that sellers want three things:

- Best/premium price
- A quick sale
- As little inconvenience and as much privacy as possible

All three! Unfortunately, we are into inconsistency almost straight away. The best price may come from someone not immediately identifiable and only "publicity" will find that person.

Often the desire for the best price will preclude the possibility of a quick sale. You may have to wait.

And third, the desire for privacy (no publicity and no inconvenience) is challenged by the advantages advertising brings.

Who are these potential purchasers and how do agents find the right ones? Some will already be known to the real estate agents, whose job it is to know what specific purchasers are looking for. Yet, there are others who are just swinging into purchaser profile, just thinking about it tentatively, and carefully driving through neighbourhoods –just watch how many cars slow down as soon as they see a "For Sale" sign. In the early stages of considering buying, they will casually skim through real estate advertisements and, as they become more determined, the skimming turns to looking carefully. The graduation from "John Citizen" to a real live committed purchaser is also an emotional transition.

So here we have sellers who have decided that it is time to sell their property which is full of memories and their feeling of security and well being. This very property that was called their own. Protected and guarded. A bastion to be transferred to a stranger with all rights to be surrendered! Not everyone, of course. Some can't wait for something better. In fact, the next property may have already been secured. Now their current home becomes a discard. The mental transfer has already happened. However, in this case, there may be the extra emotional baggage of financial trauma if an acceptable price cannot be achieved in their sale.

In case you thought you, the seller, were the only person having to go through this emotional roller coaster ride, in comes the potential purchaser. Often not sure, scared of the probable debt. Will this be the right decision for the family? Could there be something more suitable? If we like it, will we "get it" or will we suffer the disappointment (and pain) of having it go to someone else?

Little wonder that a successful real estate practitioner should be a good listener. They need to be, to be of any use!

Little wonder that amid all this indecision, many sellers warm to the suggestion that they should settle for selling with a high asking price and then allow real estate agents to bring possible purchasers already known to the agent to inspect the property. No fuss!

But that doesn't always achieve all ambitions. Some properties are easier to value than others – "Beauty is in the eye of the beholder" – and I've addressed this in more detail in the next chapter. "What price?" is a huge question.

How do you know when you've achieved an excellent price – particularly in a changing market? You may have comparable sales but do you want to try for a premium price or be content with the pattern of values that have been established?

If the market is currently good, do you want to ensure you sell before any change? If the market is not good, do you wait and, if so, for how long? Some properties require more potential purchasers than just those known to the agent before a sale can be effected. Very often the local agent does not know of the eventual buyer until that buyer responds to an advertisement or attends the open home of that property.

Many different scenarios — and that's just about the property difference! Now let's look at some of the different circumstances in which sellers may find themselves.

A transfer to a different place may mean time is not on your side. A family resettlement that means leaving a family home that is now too large or too small puts significantly less pressure on the time equation. As I've said earlier, if you've bought another home, then you don't have the luxury of time to sell your current property.

I've talked of all this not to confuse you but rather so you can realise that you are not alone in feeling almost overwhelmed with the emotion and necessary decisions that will have to be made in this process. Now you've identified with these issues, read on and let's answer your questions and concerns. I've written this book in the sequence of selling events as they may occur and given the relevant information chronologically.

What will our journey entail?

The hardest — but most important — starting point for an owner is to decide what they want. Once the key priorities are decided, it becomes apparent which selling programme will apply to them.

As sellers' key desires are rarely mutually supportive, we will be asking you to rank your key priorities between yourselves – discuss them before calling in an agent. Ranking your priorities and being able to express that ranking to your prospective agents will make a huge difference in the selling strategy you adopt. It will keep you, the seller, in charge of the process. You won't find yourself victim to a persuasive agent who assumes automatically that he or she knows what you want and what is best for you.

After these "wants" have been prioritised, you will now need as many facts and as much information as possible to make an informed decision regarding strategy and, most importantly, the choice of agent.

Then there are other issues that may arise.

Issues such as:

- What may happen during the sale?
- Can good presentation improve the sale price?
- To open or not to open your home for inspection?
- Will advertising be effective?

Contracts? Negotiation? What do I do?

I have then detailed some special circumstances, probably only applying to a minority of sellers, but very important circumstances that require individual treatment.

Finally, there are six real-life stories of different situations that may help you with your deliberation. The purpose of this book is to give you the confidence and information that will allow you to select the strategy that is right for you.

Let's Help You to Choose...

I have said that virtually all sellers want the golden three outcomes when they sell. The problems of sellers often stem from a lack of understanding of the necessity of ranking those three desired results in order of importance.

Of course, you want all three. But can you rank them in importance? If you can, it helps enormously in your decision-making process. Your final choice of strategy is easier to choose when you know what outcomes are particularly important to you.

Just to remind you of the sellers' three "wants":

- Best possible price
- Shortest time
- Least inconvenience/preservation of privacy

First, let's expand on each of these desires. What do they realistically mean when we are selling?

VERY BEST POSSIBLE PRICE

What do I mean by very best possible price? This certainly opens a vigorous discussion!

In my experience there are two prices:

a) **Vendor "happy" price**

   Many vendors are really happy with a "fair" price. They have checked the neighbourhood. They don't want to undersell. There becomes a price range with which they are "happy". Phrases are used such as "I know that I have been offered a reasonable price"; "That suits me"; "Little inconvenience (didn't need to open the home for inspection)"; "I'm happy that selling my home is now all behind me"; "It was a quick sale".

   I am not suggesting that they sold for a bargain! But the niggling question doesn't arise in these sellers' minds – "would someone else have paid more"? Or, "Was that the very best possible price?"

b) **Very best possible price**

   Sellers often think: "I want to satisfy myself that this is the very best price that is available. The best that we can possibly get."

   We call this price the market premium figure. In buoyant times, this figure could be well above what the seller may have actually dreamed of! A record. In tougher times, it may be even less than the seller had feared – but, at the time of signing, the seller was satisfied that they couldn't do better.

SHORTEST TIME

Selling a house is not always a bundle of fun. If you always have your home looking like an advertisement for *Vogue Living*, then this won't concern you as much. So often when a sale has been completed the owner will say: "Thank goodness, we can now live normally and not have to wake up every morning and make sure everything is in place." It is an effort (for most!)

Many sellers simply hate the uncertainty of not knowing what is likely to happen in the near future. Suddenly, we are not sure how long we are going to be living here. How come people don't seem to want this house we have so beautifully turned into a gorgeous home? Is it the price? Is it the agent? Is it the property? Is it us?

Tension builds. Generally this happens when the early expectation of activity is not being realised.

But then other pressures may be building. There are situations where you may have already bought and time becomes critical. Where transfers are involved, speed of sale often becomes the dominant requirement. The alternative is so often leaving one half of the family to supervise the sale (very difficult for that party). In this case, a speedy sale suits everyone. If the property is left empty, it provides its own set of problems. Where a property is empty, the shortest time on the market is desirable because no matter how diligent you are with mowing the lawns, watering the garden, "airing" it, a home empty for some time gets that unwanted "feel".

Your agent should have access to "days on market" information. Days on market are the average number of days a property takes to sell – from signing the selling agreement to finalising the contract. Of course, this information is only an "average" and this average will vary according to the selling method that you choose. It will also vary from area to area.

Different strategies impact on "days on market". If speed of sale is important then the attending agent will have already defined the time implications inherent in the different selling strategies.

LEAST INCONVENIENCE/ MOST PRIVACY

- "I don't want to be inconvenienced."
- "I want to retain my privacy; I don't even want the neighbours to know."
- "I don't want any publicity."

It is possible that these may be your most important criteria. Too often agents are obsessed with price and assume that every seller must get the best possible price. They don't LISTEN to what the owner really wants. It needs to be recognised that price is sometimes not the top criteria.

Some years ago, I received a call from a very frustrated salesperson in one of our offices in a provincial city in Queensland. She was selling the home of a very good friend of mine, a doctor with a large personal following. He refused to have a "For Sale" sign or any identifying advertising. I was asked to call and use my powers of persuasion "to make him see sense and to advise that he must auction as it's in a prime position", to quote the salesperson. On making the call he explained his position. He was not in a hurry to sell and had recently taken a partner into the practice and, as in all country cities, rumours abounded that he was going to leave the practice. The rumours were true but had he put a sign on his home, patients may have transferred to other doctors and his practice would have decreased in value. So getting the top price was not the major criteria in this case. A "quiet sale", which rarely gives the best possible price, suited this person and his circumstances. His practice was worth more than the difference in the sale prices of his home. **Privacy counted more than price** and speed of sale was not essential.

I remember another occasion where a couple were "owner building" only two doors from their own home. They needed the money from their current home to finance the building but were reluctant to move too far away from their new project – they needed to check on sub-contractors etc. daily. We had two offers on the property, one from someone who wanted to live in the house and offered a 60-day settlement. The other offer came from an investor who offered $10,000 less, a seven-day settlement and a nominal rental for the four months they estimated it would take to complete their new home. On paper the first seemed the best offer but, on analysis, looking at the convenience of no move, no changing of school for the children and the ability to continue close supervision, the second was more acceptable. It suited the investor with less outlay and the ability to negatively gear for the first year. As is the case in all successful transactions, it was a win-win situation. **Convenience counted more than price.**

So you see privacy and convenience may rank ahead of the "market premium". Are there things that are more important to YOU than top price?

As explained above, these three desires are rarely compatible. That is, it's very difficult to achieve all three – although I have included in our case studies the story of one vendor who did! (See Case Study No. 6.) You can be lucky and get all three of those components but if this is to happen you'll know VERY quickly as with no signs, no advertising, no open homes etc. you are relying on the agent already knowing of the likely buyer.

Can you work out what's most important for YOU and then rank them as on the next page? If you cannot, then it is likely that your selling experience will be frustrating and contain unnecessary reality shocks.

At this stage it is imperative that you put time and thought into defining and ranking your desires in order of priority to you.

Rank these three desires in order of priority:

☐   Best possible price

☐   Shortest time

☐   Privacy/least inconvenience and no publicity

- Is obtaining a premium price your most important criteria?
- Is it necessary, for whatever reason, to get a sale in a defined and short period of time?
- Are you more concerned with protecting your privacy and selling with the least inconvenience, than with either of the above?

Think about it before reading on.

The time that you take right now to think and then prioritise what's most important to you, will determine how happy and satisfied you will be at the conclusion of the sale. This choice will reveal to you which selling strategy will be ideal for you in contrast with one that will merely frustrate you. Choosing the method of sale that suits your priorities is of utmost importance at this time.

Now you've prioritised, find your chosen combination among the next seller profiles, read and inwardly digest! Do you really need to read the profiles that are not relevant to your situation? Maybe not.

SELLER PROFILE A

If your ranking in order of importance is...

1	**Best possible price**
2	Shortest time
3	Privacy/least inconvenience and no publicity

This seller wants the premium price – "satisfied I couldn't possibly do better" – and is prepared to do all that is necessary to get it. He or she is not at all worried about inconvenience or publicity. Timing is more important than inconvenience/publicity.

So the premium price is most important. The key question is whether to take the property to the market with the premium price set and announced, or to take it to the market without a price.

Taking it to the market with a public premium price means your agent will be dealing (at the start) with potential buyers who immediately react, "that is a very high price". That is a situation familiar to most agents. A premium asking price often immediately creates a negative response with buyers, inhibiting the development of not only an emotional attachment to the property but even preventing them seeing it. The first few weeks of selling are critical and it is important that the balance between a price that will *attract* buyers and a price that will *deter* buyers is determined at this time.

Let's Help You to Choose...

This is a situation where marketing without a price should be seriously considered. This way the buyers commit to a price before you, the seller, need to react. So, if you are going for a premium price, don't frighten away the buyers by disclosing that ambition; it's probably best to remove the price altogether. You are then able to "listen" to the market before deciding how firmly you will drive your premium price expectation.

Marketing without a price invariably results in the auction or tender process. An advertising budget is required and the property will be open for inspection (since privacy is the least important factor). The key task will be to find a number of buyers and allow competition to give you the chance of a premium price. Certainly, if the advertising budget is sufficient, it could well find "out-of-district" buyers that often set new price levels when they move into an area new to them.

The price and time priorities were brought home to me with the very first auction that I conducted as an auctioneer. The salesperson briefed me a few days before the auction and the news wasn't good! The owner was adamant that he would not sell below $90,000. While buyers coming through talked mid to late $70s, the reserve was set at $90,000 (surprise, surprise!). Very nervously, I started the auction. Eventually the bidding reached $78,000. I approached the owner, but he wasn't interested at that price so I passed the property in to be offered to the highest bidder at the reserve price. The bidder wouldn't pay more so it was back to the vendor who, to my absolute horror, said he would now withdraw the property from sale. I felt that maybe my career as an auctioneer was going to be VERY brief. He then explained that he was interested in purchasing a business, but unless he could get $90,000 or very close, he couldn't proceed with that venture and would therefore not sell his house. He thanked Carol (the salesperson) and myself profusely, explaining that in three-and-a-half weeks he had, with the increased activity of the auction, established "fair market value". It just so happened that it wasn't enough for him to go ahead with his new venture. He felt the advertising money was well spent. As he said, if he had marketed it with a price, he may have established what someone wouldn't pay ($90,000). But it would have taken much longer to find out what someone <u>would</u> pay, as the $75,000 to $80,000 buyers probably would not have even considered looking at his property. No sale, but a very satisfied customer.

So price and time were of equal importance to him. While no sale was achieved, the exercise was successful. He realised that his very important premium price couldn't be achieved and he found that out in the shortest possible time.

Seller Profile A recommendation:

You will probably find that an auction with an advertising budget that identifies your property will suit you best. If you are in an area where you feel this option may not be at all appropriate, than market with a premium price. Advertising is the best support you can give to your ambition for a premium price.

SELLER PROFILE B

If your choice is...

1	Privacy/least inconvenience and no publicity
2	Shortest time
3	Best possible price

The highest priority for non-inconvenience/privacy with the least interest in price is, as you might imagine, unusual and generally involves some special circumstances. Christopher Skase sold his Brisbane mansion in 24 hours, in maximum secrecy and fled! Privacy and time was obviously more important than price! But there are many other honorable situations when the circumstances dictating the decision to sell are so intense and painful that the desire is, "get me out of here". Even opening for inspection is not on. Here the "vendor happy" price is all the sellers are thinking of – indeed they could well be prepared to take a bargain price to get it all behind them. (I know many people won't believe me, but agents hate selling for bargain prices, even when vendors don't care and just want out. It's not what we pride ourselves in achieving.)

Probably neither open homes nor any advertising that might identify your property will be chosen. Possibly you may even decide against a "For Sale" sign.

In this case, do you have one agent or do you have it listed with lots of agents? If agents sense that price is relatively unimportant for a seller, there is sure to be an intensity of activity as they contact buyers. All buyers love bargains and it's amazing how buyers' priorities change dramatically and become unimportant if a property is really keenly priced.

But if your privacy requirements are really essential, you may not want to have to communicate with a lot of agents. A sole agent would be ideal – far more private. Be sure that you select an agent that will be active and recognise that time is also important to you.

> **Seller Profile B recommendation:**
>
> *A sole/exclusive agency with a price will retain your privacy and if the agent cannot immediately identify a buyer then you may need advertising that does not identify your house, yet refers to the attractive price. Alternatively you could also ask your agent to have just one "open house by invitation only" where his/her current buyers could be asked to inspect your home at one designated time (no signs, just privately invited). If this doesn't result in a sale then you will need to revert to non-identifying advertising.*

SELLER PROFILE C

If your selected choice is...

1	**Best possible price**
2	Privacy/least inconvenience and no publicity
3	Shortest time

Our sellers want to get the best possible price but want least inconvenience and privacy – "we have plenty of time to sell". Time is not a priority. Many sellers are in this category. In fact, if you asked all sellers to rank their priorities, our guess is that the majority would select this combination.

Many of these sellers' willingness to offer their property to possible purchasers would have been initiated by an agent contacting the owner with: "If I got you a really good price, would you sell?" Here we have a relatively non-committed vendor who, if no attractive offer is forthcoming, will be happy to stay living and owning the property. Their only reason for selling would be the premium price offered. They are not interested in advertising in any shape or form, don't want to be inconvenienced and speed of sale doesn't even enter the equation - this is almost the perfect sale for any owner!

It goes like this: "We have time on our side, so we can wait for a premium price; "We're not in a hurry"; "Hopefully, the agent will find the right buyer and, with his negotiating skills, bring about a premium price".

Very logical. Many agents wrestle with what advice to give in these circumstances. The temptation is to list the property with a premium price and hope that the perfect buyer will "come". Perhaps your agent is already talking to the perfect buyer. But what if they balk at the price? How do the agents keep finding new prospects while maintaining privacy – particularly if time is unimportant and the sales process becomes drawn out?

With this profile, you may not have wanted or accepted the idea of a specific advertising plan. However, your agent may well be reluctant to spend some of their own money publicising your property under these circumstances. At some stage, activity starts to slow. As activity slackens so do your chances of getting the best price. It may be necessary in those circumstances to consider embarking on a planned advertising programme if they really wish to sell.

Due to the relative importance of privacy, using one sole agent will be beneficial for you – especially an agent who understands your desire for a premium price and privacy. As the sales process continues, how do you review the premium price ambition? Is time still as unimportant? Time may not have featured prominently in the early stages of marketing but, as the weeks go by, frustration sets in and the speed of sale becomes important.

So the desire of sellers to secure the premium price may gradually overcome their concerns about inconvenience and privacy. An advertising campaign, combined with open homes, would now give confidence to the seller that a more determined effort is being made to find the right purchasers. This happens when the seller is now not so sanguine about the time being taken. Waiting is no longer as attractive as doing something positive. The most positive thing that one can do is to be proactive in inviting potential purchasers to come directly to your home using the open home method. This is easier now that more and more purchasers are going to open for inspections' properties rather than first going to a real estate agent. At this stage you may even decide, rather than publicly reduce the price in order to effect a sale, that you will remove the price and offer the property by auction. The sacrifice of some of the "privacy" may be worth the opportunity of achieving a premium price. Remember that you CAN change strategies if your priorities change.

At this time vendors often regret not being more active in advertising the property at the early time of listing when it would have had the advantage of a property fresh to the market.

Seller Profile C recommendation:

Certainly start the process by listing at a premium price with one agent in order to keep your privacy. Be prepared to change strategies if necessary to achieve the premium price and even to forgo some privacy. If the above strategy doesn't effect a satisfactory sale, reconsider your selling strategy and again consider non-identifying advertising that still protects your privacy but may attract buyers.

SELLER PROFILE D

If this is your order of priority...

1	Privacy/least inconvenience and no publicity
2	Best possible price
3	Shortest time

Our sellers here have the same overwhelming desire for privacy as our sellers in Profile B. But now, price is more important than it was then. Now, time is least important. Perhaps the emotional circumstances being experienced by our sellers are not as intense. Again, maybe the overriding desire for privacy is more a reflection of the seller's personality than any specific circumstances that led to the decision to sell. However, the greater desire for a premium price (than seller profile B) leads to some significant issues. It raises the question of marketing with or without a price.

You can market with or without a price. Due to the relatively higher importance of a premium price, sellers will be more interested in a marketing campaign that incurs the least inconvenience. An often adopted technique for these sellers is for their property to be advertised with no "open for inspection" arrangements, and no address, with enquiries being directed to the agent – who will qualify purchasers before undertaking a personal inspection with them.

An exclusive agent will be the preferred appointment. Some sellers with this profile don't even want a "FOR SALE'" sign on their property, fearing unwanted attention from their neighbourhood.

Thus, if your desire for privacy is such that you will not even consider identifying advertising or a sign, you will need to be patient. With no advertising or signage, it may take some time to effect a sale at an acceptable price. You must realise that you are really, in effect, waiting for a suitable buyer to "walk in" to the office or for your agent to stumble across someone wanting your property and willing to pay a price acceptable to you.

One danger of a selling campaign where privacy is the overwhelming requirement and yet premium price remains a key ambition is that, as time passes, sellers often become frustrated. Hopefully, that frustration does not lead to the seller suddenly sacrificing "price" to the point of accepting a "bargain price".

Seller profile D recommendation:

Appoint one agent and market with or without a price. If the lack of activity becomes too frustrating you may need to review your priorities or your asking price (or both!).

SELLER PROFILE E

Maybe this suits you best...

1	Shortest time
2	Best possible price
3	Privacy/least inconvenience and no publicity

You want action. You don't care about inconvenience and you don't want the price to be sacrificed, but speed is the overriding consideration.

It can happen for all types of reasons. Not just transfers or another purchase but just the personality of the sellers. "I've made up my mind to sell. And I want to get on with it. Yet I don't want to sacrifice a premium price opportunity."

Sometimes, the decision to sell is made after months of questioning, but once the decision is made, the sellers here are ready for action. These sellers really respond to promotion and marketing without a price. "Let's promote the availability of this property to as wide a range of buyers as possible."

This is what all frustrated buyers are continually looking for – brand new listings!

Almost certainly, here you will be supporting newspaper advertising, with the property opened for inspection. If the price is removed, this lack of the published price expectation as the dominant priority will result in a better chance of buyers becoming emotionally attached to the property before price becomes a hindrance or a problem. People viewing the property will be forced to compare and judge the property on the *merits* of the property, not on the *price* quoted. "We want this property – now what is the maximum price I can either afford or be comfortable in paying."

Most likely this campaign will result in an auction (which is just another term for bringing interest to a head within a specific time frame).

Here, you will be increasing and broadening interest by removing the price. In doing so you are increasing the opportunity to achieve a premium price. The overriding priority, speed of sale, is also achieved with the "urgency" that an auction promotes in buyers.

The key here is marketing without a price. Price has been removed as an impediment to the timing process. Yet, the expectation of a premium price has been maintained. Certainly, at the end of the campaign, you should be able to say, "I believe I have achieved the best possible price that is available" – our definition of premium price.

The whole campaign from agent selection to sale of the property could be as little as one month to six weeks. In fact, it could be less if time is really critical. This could be dependent on the exposure and content of the advertising campaign selected.

Here's a story ...

I had the situation when someone was transferred and wanted a sale before he left 10 days later. I checked to see if anyone in the office already had a buyer who could be interested, with no success – except for those who had a buyer who would be interested in a "bargain". As getting an acceptable price was fairly high on his list of priorities, selling at a bargain price was NOT an option, so we talked "auction" and decided that the urgency of this situation could be used to his advantage. So, on the following Saturday, there was a prominent ad and photo that couldn't be missed. The heading said it all: "If you're in a hurry to buy, this owner is in a hurry to sell. SEVEN-DAY AUCTION." It created huge interest. We "opened" it each day and auctioned it the following Saturday, and as is nearly always the case where there are multiple buyers, the property sold above reserve and the owner was on his way. Of course, this wouldn't work in every situation but the need dictated the circumstances.

> **Seller Profile E recommendation:**
>
> *The method most likely to achieve these goals is auction with an advertising budget to broaden the range of buyers viewing the property. It could be marketed with an exclusive/sole agency and without a price, but the importance of timing will be better satisfied by the auction process.*

SELLER PROFILE F

When our seller wants...

1	Shortest time
2	Privacy/least inconvenience and no publicity
3	Best possible price

The sellers who fit this profile may have already experienced the selling process before and been frustrated by all sorts of issues. "I don't want to get caught again"; I don't want the uncertainty this time of not knowing when I am going to get this sale behind me", and so on.

Nevertheless, the importance of privacy could mean a reluctance to have open home inspections and even advertising. The lower ranking of price means the sellers will be prepared to have the reasonable price expectation presented as the major advantage for potential buyers. In this case, appointing one agent will probably be appropriate and the advertising will no doubt concentrate on the value of the property.

As with the decision for privacy, the importance of buyer activity could well encourage the support of an advertising campaign – particularly if problems in selling before related to buyer inactivity. Here, any advertising is more likely to have "inspection by appointment". Perhaps the element of speed will negate privacy ambitions so that open for inspections may even be considered in order to achieve the widest coverage. A sole agency will be important to maintain control and the privacy our sellers want. Possibly fulfilling the first two desires will probably inhibit a high price outcome.

> **Seller Profile F recommendation:**
>
> *If premium price is not as important as your desire for speed of sale and privacy, then an exclusive/sole agency would be preferred with an advertising plan concentrating on the attractive price/outstanding value. You will probably prefer that the advertising does not identify your property with an address.*

SUMMARY

I have tried to define many of the different circumstances you may experience when selling.

I believe the best strategies can only be developed once you know the priorities of your critical elements.

What sometimes happens is that circumstances change during the campaign and so your priorities can change. Probably the most common change is a change of priority for the speed of the sale (see case study no. 5). Again and again a property is put on the market with speed of sale not a contributing factor then – guess what – the seller finds a property that they "love". Whether they buy it or just hope "no one else does before they are in a position to secure it", suddenly "shortest time" jumps to the top of the priority list.

Perhaps the price of the next property you want means that it becomes more important to achieve the premium price for your home. Perhaps that was not as important before. Perhaps you lose your concerns for privacy – "I'll now do whatever is necessary" and so on.

When this happens please, please take your agent into your confidence. If selling with a price, you may decide to reduce the price in order to attract new buyers. If you do decide to do this, ask your agent to contact everyone who has already seen your home (and hasn't yet bought) and advise them of the new price. You may get one or two of them back again for a second inspection. Sometimes, agents don't remember to do this.

Just remember changed circumstances probably mean a changed strategy.

Some estate agents only want to sell your home one way.

Not Ray White.

Fortunately, Ray White understands the options.

We know that to ensure the premium price, there are different ways to sell your home. Some estate agents ignore the fact that all homes are different and every seller has different needs. They only want to sell your home one way: their way. (Perhaps to give them more time on the golf course).

After 100 years in real estate, Ray White knows the best method for you.

We have 60,000 satisfied customers every year who agree with us.

They appreciate getting a premium price for their home with Australia's favourite real estate agent, Ray White.

Wouldn't you?

Ray White
REAL ESTATE

Selling Methods Explained

Hopefully, the previous chapter has assisted in the prioritising of your needs. It is important to know what exactly is involved in the different selling methods.

I call this the "how" of the process – "how" will you sell your home and "how" does it work?

Perhaps the most important question is to decide between selling:

1. WITH A PRICE

2. WITHOUT A PRICE

One thing to closely look at is the traditional types of selling methods currently being used in the area where you live. In some areas, most properties are open for inspection with a marketing campaign in a major newspaper. In other areas, properties are advertised in the local newspaper. It makes good sense to see what your potential buyers are used to. Sometimes, of course, being different can take you out of the pack.

There are some very good techniques that are not used frequently because the market doesn't understand them or is not comfortable with them. Tenders are a good example of this. We have seen cases where tenders work brilliantly with residential property, but, in the main, they're not often recommended, as buyers are not generally familiar with how they work.

WITH A PRICE

If you've decided to market with a price, then the decision about what figure you will take your property to the market with is one of the most critical in the whole selling program. Pricing property can be difficult. At this point, it is useful to know which seller profile is yours. How important is the premium price against a "vendor happy" price?

At the outset, it is really useful if you can do your own homework on the market. This will be helpful to you when you finally call in the real estate agent. There are two issues in your mind — what am I likely to finally want for the property and what will be the right price to take it to the market?

Much is written and spoken about in terms of the price at which vendors should list their property. Certainly, if you are listing with a price, invariably purchasers seeking to negotiate will test that price. By far the greater number of transactions in this way result from some negotiation from the vendor regarding price. So, do you list at 5% above your expected figure? Or 10%? What's the best way to do your homework?

- Visiting open for inspections is ideal. Not only does it give you an idea of the competition your own property will be meeting, but you are also able to find out asking prices. The attendant agent should be able to give recent sales figures etc.

- Remember, if talking to sellers who have sold, there is a great temptation to exaggerate what they got for their properties – it's called "selective amnesia".

- If auctions are being held in your trade area, visiting those will be productive. It will also give you the experience of witnessing the procedure of marketing without a price.

- Very often, "sold" signs will appear in your trade area. Ring the agent for details.

- There are also some good information centres where sales results recorded by different government departments are published.

The big thing to remember is that, at the end of the day, the sale prices have all come about because there has been a purchaser prepared to pay that figure. So, the more preparation you do, the more confidence you will have in your price range.

For a real estate agent, there will be the task of recommending a price to you. When you realise that listings are the lifeblood of real estate agents, few agents will wish to risk the chance of being your agent because they've mishandled the whole price issue. Therefore, agents will be attempting to secure your favour by offering an attractive expected price. In some cases, particularly when a long sole/exclusive agency can be arranged, agents won't mind a ridiculously high starting price because the agent will hope that, with a long sole agency period, the seller will adopt a lower price before his agreement runs out.

I have two stories which indicate how agents need to understand some subtle benefits different properties may have and also the times when estate agents can get emotionally involved and over-assess the value of a property.

> For example, I sat in the Hyatt Hotel in Perth one evening and watched the sun set over the Swan River. It was just the most magnificent sight one could ever imagine. The sky changed from red to gold and the colours were reflected on the expanse of the river, and on the buildings, and as night gradually took over the lights came on - truly an absolutely enchanting scene. I imagined what joy the owners of homes along the Swan River must experience every evening.

> During that day the training group I was leading had discussed the problems associated with setting prices on property. I had expressed the opinion that real estate agents weren't always correct in their opinion of market value and in fact (horror of horrors!) sometimes the owners might even be correct! Vehemently, the salespeople had told me that you <u>could</u> compare properties and so arrive at a "true and correct" figure.

Selling Methods Explained

> *As I watched the sunset, I thought to myself: "How much do you add on for a sunset?" – $1000? $5000. $500? Or is the house worth less, because it faces west?*
>
> *Who can price a sunset?*

Buying a house is a totally emotional experience and the decision and price paid will be made on emotional issues. So, next time you're tempted to think of an agent as a "pricer" of a property instead of a "marketer", just ask yourself: How much is a sunset worth?

Some agents may not put value on a "sunset" and so, in essence, possibly suggest too low a price, but the opposite can also be the case. The suggested price might even be too HIGH! For example, I was called in to look at a property that the owners wanted to sell.

> *Talk about enthusiasm; I absolutely fell in love with it. It was my type of house, so pretty with french windows, velvet curtains and roses over the entry. Can't you see it? Can even remember the ad that I wrote. The heading was "Pretty as a picture" and started off "and situated on the top of a hill to catch every breeze". I loved the house and couldn't imagine that everyone wouldn't pay practically **anything** for it. After the first ad appeared in the paper, reality set in. Time and again, I heard the comment: "It's a commission house with french doors." "Commission" in Queensland refers to state-built houses. I then committed the next sin for a real estate agent - I defended the house with "but look at the curtains and the roses"! It didn't impress all those buyers who*

45

still said *"it's a commission house with french doors"*. Hat in hand, I approached the owners with the news that while they loved the house and I loved the house, the *"buyers weren't as excited as we were"*. It took a couple of weeks before we both realised that there needed a major re-adjustment of price if the property was to sell. In this case, the agent falling in love with the house probably wasted at least one week, maybe two, of good marketing time. The "market" is more important than the agent. The postscript to the above is that eventually I found a buyer who loved the roses, french doors etc. but we <u>still</u> had to negotiate to get the sale together. And I couldn't believe it when, during negotiation, they said: *"It really is just a commission house with french doors."* I knew that my enthusiasm for the house would eventually sell it, but it was important that I, as well as the owners, listened to what the market said.

So how <u>do</u> you decide at what price you should put your home on the market? With great difficulty, and without doubt, real estate agents agonise over this question more than any other.

All you have to help you is a comparative market analysis, your agent's "gut" feeling and your own ideas.

COMPARATIVE MARKET ANALYSIS (CMA)

This is where the agent supplies a list, brief description and selling price of properties around your price range that have sold lately. Of course, you must take the state of the market into account when you view these figures as most will, of necessity, be at least a couple of months old. Unless the property is sold at public auction those figures are confidential until they have been through the relevant government department. And, of course, because you're dealing with a government department, you can wait quite a few weeks and sometimes months. So if the market has gone down, you'll need to realise that the chances are your property will not get as much as that analysis would suggest. By the same token, if the market has gone up, you will need to estimate how much more you can get for your property. As you can understand, pricing a property is not an exact science. Comparative market analysis gives a rough guide only as every home has some differences. Too often with these figures, sellers end up comparing apples with oranges!

Agent's "gut feeling" - Well, if a CMA is not an exact science then neither is an agent's feeling. Of course, an agent has an idea of a range, but I doubt if there is an agent who hadn't at sometime been surprised at the price some property achieved. It can only be a guide.

What you want - Remember no matter what the CMA shows or the agent says, **you** have the final choice about at what price the property will be marketed. All our research shows that a property has the greatest chance of a sale in the first three to four weeks of marketing! Unless premium price is your first priority with speed of sale of little or no consequence, you must be aware of the possibility that your "want" price may deter rather than attract the eventual buyer.

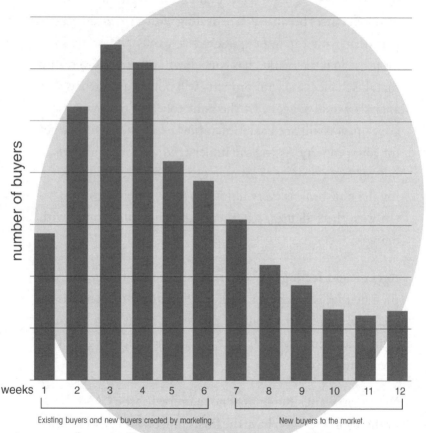

These figures have been collated from figures obtained from Ray White offices in every state of Australia and both North and South islands of New Zealand.

Selling Methods Explained

Why are the first few weeks so significant? The "active span" of a buyer is assessed at five to six weeks – according to industry statistics, the average buyer spends five to six weeks after they enter the market fully qualified and ready to buy before they make a decision on a property. You and I know people who have taken months and months to decide, but they are balanced out by the people who buy the second or third (sometimes the very first) house they see! So, every time a new property becomes available, every (nearly every) buyer is aware of new signs in their preferred area. Immediately there is interest by the backlog (average five to six weeks) of buyers. After the first few weeks of your marketing most of this backlog will have seen your property and have either put in an offer or dismissed it. From then on there are just the new buyers who come into the market each week.

If the decision is to market with a price, there are several methods that you can use:

- Sell it yourself
- Open or general listing
- Multi-list
- Exclusive listing

I will explain the difference in the strategies later in this chapter.

WITHOUT A PRICE

Some properties are relatively easy to price because there are obvious comparables. Where there are multiple differences whether it is size, construction or area of land, pricing becomes a very inaccurate science. For example, how much is a sunset worth?

Marketing without a price gives the owner more time before a decision has to be made as to the eventual market price. It also gives the owner more information from potential buyers, unprompted by any suggested price. I have seen sellers who have sought a premium price, been over-optimistic with those expectations and then lost all confidence in those same expectations. They have then often overreacted by sometimes bringing that premium asking price down to almost a bargain.

By marketing without a price you force the buyers to judge your property on the merits of the property rather than on the merits of the price. With no price the buyers decide whether or not they are interested in the property, based solely on the property. If they're interested, then the agent's job is to get a price that is satisfactory to both parties.

You can market without a price by using the following methods:

- Exclusive agency
- Auction
- Tender

Now let's discuss the technicalities of each selling method.

SELL IT YOURSELF

Selling your home yourself is an option available to everyone.

We recently did a survey over some months that involved staff from corporate offices phoning private sellers with a series of questions as to why they had decided to sell their home themselves. We continued surveying the same people over several months to monitor results. The results were so definite that one can only assume that the trend shown would not differ whenever or wherever we surveyed.

We found that most people made the decision to try to sell it themselves. Not to save commission (as thought), but because they either couldn't find a real estate person in whom they had confidence or trust or their past experience with a real estate person had been unsatisfactory – a sad indictment on the industry. BUT there are good real estate agents if you will just go through the process of selection carefully.

Of those surveyed, only one person successfully sold their home themselves so I called on the lady and explained our research and asked if she'd mind telling me the story. First of all, a young couple really liked the house but hadn't organised finance and so persuaded the owner to wait until they did so. She waited three weeks before they then told her that they'd "changed their minds"! After another couple of weeks she was approached by another gentleman who offered her considerably less than what she was asking, and after she'd eventually and reluctantly agreed, he had his solicitor draw up a contract which she duly signed. Only after signing and then reading (ALWAYS read before you sign anything) did she discover the settlement was not for four months! This was most inconvenient for her as she was moving interstate. It was not a happy experience for her. I didn't have the heart to tell her that, from what I'd seen of the house, she'd probably sold it considerably under market value.

It's not because I want to keep real estate agents in work but I cannot recommend that you sell your own property. Buyers who buy privately do so because they believe they'll get it cheaper – (as above) and they often do! Agents are trained to negotiate fairly and it's so much easier to work through a third party.

Would you really be able to deal with emotional situations when confronted face to face with the buyer? Would you really be able to tell that lovely young couple who really wanted the house because it was close to their invalid parents that they'd have to find another $5000 and that they can't have the outdoor furniture? Would you be a match for the seasoned investor who tried to PROVE to you that his offer of $10,000 less than you wanted was the best you'd ever get? The agent becomes the almost anonymous person who is able to present the opinions of both parties in a more bipartisan atmosphere.

In my experience, I've found that the majority of genuine buyers are uncomfortable even looking at homes when the owners are there – let alone when the owner shows them through. Genuine buyers prefer to deal through the agent so the majority of people who will contact "private" sellers are either "lookers" or very experienced buyers who are determined to get a bargain. The inexperienced seller is no match for the latter and so undersells their property. Don't let this happen to you – it's not worth the effort.

Find an agent in whom you have confidence. With our survey, we found that most of the remaining owners eventually gave their property to a real estate agent to sell. All they'd done was waste time and advertising money that could have been better invested in an agent.

OPEN OR GENERAL LISTING – (WITH A PRICE)

The terminology changes according to the area. An "open" listing is the same as a "general" listing. Again, the normal practice is to put a price on a property when sold this way.

The open/general method is when owners ask three or four (or more!) agents to all try to sell their home. This method has gone out of favour, as ways of selling have become more sophisticated. The theory of giving it to everyone is that the competition between the agents to get a sale will result in increased activity. In reality, this doesn't happen unless the property is priced so low that it's easy to sell.

Then, some people will say (or think): "I don't want to exclude any buyers." If you gathered together a group of agents and asked them to name the top five buyers with whom they were working, you'd find the same names appearing again and again. A correctly marketed property will be seen by the buyers in the marketplace. Have you ever heard of a buyer who says: "I won't look at that property as it's not listed with the agent I've been dealing with?" Of course not.

An unfortunate accompaniment to the "open" listing is the plethora of signs of these properties. They look untidy and just scream desperation. Buyers ask "What's the matter with the property?"

MULTI-LIST – (WITH A PRICE)

This is a system where groups of agencies exchange listings with photos and details. It is an exclusive listing that you cannot give to another agency during that agency period. The listing agency distributes the photograph and details to other agencies within the multi-list group. Only a comparatively small group of agencies extensively use the multi-list system. This system really is a cross between an open and exclusive listing.

The theory is that by distributing these details to all the agents in the "multi-list" group, the property will be exposed to more agents. It is a pity that some agents have abused this system by feeling that their job is done once it's been distributed to the other agents. No one takes responsibility. Some agencies use this system more successfully than others do. Ask for the individual office success rate with multi-list before committing.

Across our markets, the use of multi listing is declining. There are complaints from sellers that they can't influence the way that the property is described to potential purchasers, particularly where a premium price is being sought.

Increasingly the concept is becoming less popular for all concerned.

EXCLUSIVE/SOLE AGENCY (WITH OR WITHOUT A PRICE)

An exclusive/sole agency is where just one agent is appointed.

The key component of an exclusive agency is the time period sought by that agent. Actually, the time period requested is not a bad indication of the expected time that the agent thinks he or she will need to complete a successful sale. The most usual period is from 30 to 90 days. The agency agreement is with the real estate agency. That means that, should the real estate salesperson leave during the period of engagement, the agreement will still continue with that office. You cannot breach this agreement during this period. It is imperative that you check how long the agency agreement will remain in place. I must urge you again to read carefully before signing anything.

With an exclusive appointment most sellers value the relationship they develop with their chosen agent and see that as very helpful during the entire selling period. When that agent understands your needs and circumstances, only then is the advice given worthwhile. The extra effort and extra services given when you commit to one agency will provide the critical difference between a successful outcome and frustration. These services cannot be provided if an agent is appointed on an "open" basis, which is just an "opportunity" appointment rather than a "responsibility" appointment. With an open appointment the agent has the "opportunity" to sell the property, but with an exclusive appointment your agent accepts the "responsibility" to sell it.

Certainly, if you are taking your property to the market without a price, an exclusive agent is critical. It is just not possible to perfect the selling strategy with no price, if an exclusive agent is not appointed to manage the process for you.

Other benefits include having only one signboard, one set of keys and accurate feedback from all inspections. Using the exclusive method of appointments allows you to choose to market with or without a price.

Marketing without a price via an exclusive agency gives the advantages previously listed. This technique is used more in the upper end of the market and history has shown that it can be effective, particularly where it is difficult to establish a probable price range and where price is a major priority. Sometimes, we have found buyer resistance to homes marketed without a price and not "auctioned". Buyers seem to accept the "no price" with auction but are sometimes confused with "no price" on an exclusive listing. This method is certainly an option at your disposal and is appropriate if your priorities are price and privacy. It allows you to access the market for unsolicited information on price with the chance that the elusive emotional buyer will see your property and pay a premium price.

If you choose to sell exclusively and with a price, never forget that the price at which that property is put on the market is your choice. If premium price is your top priority you will no doubt test the market with a "top" price, while if price is lower in your priorities, you will no doubt decide on a price more likely to attract multiple buyers to your property. These are decisions that should be discussed with your agent.

AUCTION

One of the real advantages of auction is that the buyers know that the owners genuinely want to sell. Genuine buyers only want to deal with genuine sellers and genuine sellers only want to deal with genuine buyers. Buyers who are "looking" and are not ready to buy are rarely attracted to an auction, as that sense of urgency does not suit their priorities at that time. Buyers who are anxious to buy will be more attracted by auctions as the feeling that the owner is keen to sell better suits their time-frame.

Some states and territories have very involved and complicated conveyancing laws. Laws which make it difficult to ascertain exactly when a contract is binding on the purchaser – often the seller may not know until the actual exchange of contract whether the buyer is proceeding with the sale. With a property sold using an auction contract, the only terms and conditions are that there will be a 10% deposit, a defined settlement time and it will be a "cash" contract – i.e. the buyer will have organised their finance before signing. Whether or not you live in an area with these rather complicated contracts, a contract under auction conditions is probably the simplest contract for you, the seller. **Once signed, sold!**

This is an often-forgotten advantage of this method of marketing.

From my experience, I've found that one of the greatest advantages of auction is the absence of price. The absence of price will not deter genuine buyers - genuine buyers do their homework, are the true deciders of market price and **genuine buyers know value.**

Auctions obviate the need to be worried about the price. "At what price will I put it on the market?" is such a very difficult decision. If it hasn't sold at auction, at least you now have a very good idea of fair market value and at what price it would be realistic to market the property.

Through experience and hearing so many success stories, many people have become passionate about marketing without a price and the most accepted method of dispensing with price is through auction.

So often people will ask: "But how often do they get their reserve." Of course, the answer is "not always", but then, when a property is put on the market with a price, people will ask: "How often do they get that price?" The answer is "rarely". However, with auction, there is always that chance – and there is always the chance that you may get more than the reserve.

With an auction it is hoped that a number of buyers will emerge – several of whom will 'want' the property. They have already identified themselves with the property – the only problem is they have to outbid any other interested prospective purchasers before it is theirs. That is the value of this process; it brings the interest and activity to a head – or climax – at the auction itself. By now the seller will have been able to evaluate the levels of interest, and so better "fine-tune" his price expectations.

Obviously, the seller is not obliged to accept the highest offer at auction. But as our story in seller profile A in the previous chapter outlined, the seller now knows what is likely to be the best possible price anyone will pay.

Auctions contain the element of speed with the opportunity of a premium price.

Here is a story that illustrates the ability to get that elusive premium price, as well as the power of the excitement of auction day. One of our offices had been approached to give a market appraisal on a small cottage, which was on a fair-sized block of land in a suburb in Brisbane. It was owned by a lady who, after living in the cottage for 40 years, had moved to a retirement village. Her son was looking after the sale and had called in lots and lots of agents to get an idea of price. It wasn't easy as it was a well-established suburb with little or no vacant land, and really it was land value only. Guess these agents had a crystal ball, as they all said between $80,000 and $90,000. With honesty the salesperson from our office said that there was no way that she could "guess" at a price, as there were no comparable sales. Auction was chosen as the marketing method and on the morning of the auction the reserve was set for $90,000. I was at the auction and when the first bid came in at $50,000, the poor owner was absolutely distraught thinking that this was the final price. Seeing her concern, the auctioneer actually stopped the auction to explain to her that was just the FIRST bid! From then on "it was all roses", with the final bidder paying $137,500 – that's 50% more than any other agent said that they'd get. From the momentary disappointment when she thought she would only get $50,000 to the elation where she realised she'd got $137,500! The agents who recommended $80,000 to $90,000 were not trying to mislead, but they didn't consider the possibility that they might be WRONG.

Of course, not every auction finds that premium price buyer. It would be wrong to say that it does. An auction gives the best CHANCE to find that buyer.

Are there any types of homes that are more conducive to auction than others? Actually, geographic areas are often more reliable in determining selling strategies. In some areas of Australia, 50% or more of selling strategies are based on marketing without a price. In other areas it is less than 5%!

Also, different properties may elect different preferred strategies.

If you still have concerns about the pros and cons of auction, there is another chapter on "Auctions are flexible".

NOW WHAT ABOUT TENDERS

While tender is accepted in large commercial properties where there are often complicated conditions regarding zoning and use approval clauses, it is not always as widely accepted or appropriate in domestic marketplaces. A tender does not, like auction, have to be an unconditional offer. The interested buyer collects a tender document (from the selling agency) and fills in the relevant details, encloses a deposit, puts it in a sealed envelope and then places it in the "tender" box until the advertised time of "closing". Then, all tenders are opened in the presence of the property owners.

Tender is used in residential property (more likely at the top end of the market) where there may be conditional clauses (subject to re-zoning etc) or variations in payment options. The tender documents often act more as "expressions of interest" and they allow the owner to negotiate with several parties. While the market price issue does not need to be addressed, the excitement and competition of the auction are missing in tender.

One of the best examples I've seen where tender was the preferred method of marketing occurred when an order of missionaries decided to sell their beautiful retreat about one hour's drive out of Brisbane. It was important for them to know exactly who all the possible buyers were, as the graves of some of the brothers were within the grounds, and they were also concerned that the property not be bought by any fringe groups whose beliefs may not be in line with theirs. With an auction there would not be the opportunity to do searches on people or companies bidding. Then, as to price, how do you price a magnificent two-storey "mansion", detached dormitory accommodation and classrooms, all set in 100 acres of farm land and complete with a producing dairy farm. They really wanted a local (one hour's drive!) boys' non-denominational boarding school to buy it as a retreat but felt that justice must be seen to be done.

So the tenders arrived and the owner's solicitors opened the documents. I do not know the amounts offered but they did tell me that at least one "fringe group" was a tenderer and the boy's school was the successful buyer. The school had also included a clause committing itself to maintaining the graves and allowing the brothers access to that area.

This was a case where tender was really their best option and where the very best price wasn't their top priority.

With a price or without a price?

The choice really comes down to: "Will it be best to market with a price or without a price?" If you decide that a price would be most advantageous in your market then you should choose an exclusive agency programme. If, however, you can see the advantages of removing the price and creating competition, then auction is probably your best option. Ask your agent to talk about both options.

Always remember that the final choice of which strategy you will use to market your home will be your choice. Don't allow any agent to push you into a method with which you are uncomfortable. But, by the same token, do allow them to explain your selling options, so that you fully understand the choices you have before you make a decision. Any agent who does not give you a choice is not recognising that different homes and different owners have different needs.

"They can have any colour they want, as long as it's black." Henry Ford

"Private treaty, auction, tender. Our customers need options." Ray White

Some Real Estate agents are still driving T Model Fords when it comes to selling your home.

No choice, no flexibility.

At Ray White we believe that, with our expert advice and choice of options, you will achieve the highest possible price.

That's why some properties lend themselves to either private treaty, auction or tender.

Why then, do people opt for black and white when you've got the choice of colour.

Ray White Real Estate. Marketing Packages to suit all budgets.

Ray White.
REAL ESTATE

WHO? Which Agent Will Best Suit Me?

The "ability to talk" does not make a successful real estate agent. It's the "ability to listen" that makes a successful agent.

When selling I would choose an agent who asked me questions so I knew that they understood my own particular needs and circumstances. I would then expect them to listen to the answers and base their recommendations on what they've heard from me. Too often agents go in with a fixed idea of how a property should be marketed. Again, let me stress, every property is different. I would want an agent who I was positive had listened to me and had given advice on what he or she had learnt about my own situation. Always choose an agent who listens to you, not one who makes you listen to them!

There are so many tired, jaded and unenthusiastic salespeople in every area where sales are made and personally I won't deal with them. I would not be satisfied until I found a salesperson who really <u>wanted</u> to sell my home. If the salesperson isn't enthusiastic now, how will he or she be able to sell your home to a buyer? Look for the person who walks in and remarks positively about your home and certainly reject the agent who, on entering, makes negative comments. I remember when I was selling my house in Melbourne (reluctantly, but I was returning to Queensland), one agent's first remark was "It's very pink, isn't it?" Well, I like pink, and apart from the exterior, the carpet and some walls, it wasn't that pink! My reply was: "It's a woman's house. You'll never sell it to a man." When his answer was, "well, that cuts the buyers down by half", I knew he wasn't the person who could sell my house. I needed someone who was enthusiastic about pink houses and I did find her. And yes, a woman and her teenage daughter were the eventual buyers.

New salespeople are nearly always brimming with enthusiasm as they rapidly gain experience. What sometimes happens is that, as the experience level rises, so the level of enthusiasm falls. Never underestimate the power of the enthusiasm of the new salesperson. Enthusiasm so often achieves more than just experience by itself.

It may seem strange but I put personal appearance high on the list of requirements, as it tells you so much about the person. If someone's personal presentation is not acceptable to me, then I always think that their work will probably not be of an acceptable standard. Poor personal presentation reflects a person's attitude to themselves, their work and life in general. I'm not saying that they need to be dressed in designer clothes but the things that I'd look for would be:

- Always a tie and no frayed collar and cuffs
- No short, short skirts (for women) – they give the wrong message!
- No shirt tails or blouses hanging out.
- Neat, tidy and clean hair.
- Then, of course, clean shoes.

Actually, the selection of their agent is one of the more important business selections most people make in their adult lives.

Often people select an agent without really feeling confident that that agent is really "on their side". It's almost as if there is the expectation that such a situation is not likely and therefore they don't expect it.

Keep looking until you find an agent you can trust.

I would also ask to see testimonials, and if I had doubts, maybe I would even ask if I could phone a couple of those past clients. I realise that you may be uncomfortable asking this, but it is your right. When you do phone those people, focus on this question: "Did you feel Mr Agent negotiated effectively on your behalf?" A good track record is reflected in the willingness of past clients to provide testimonials. Then, of course, confidence also comes from a good track record. I always have, and always will, favour someone who lives in the area because they can sell the benefits of the area to the potential buyer.

And imagine your salesperson as the one influencing your likely buyer. Will that person present your property positively to likely purchasers? As in my case, I knew that the agent who saw my beautiful home as too pink would not talk in a manner likely to influence buyers positively. Will there be continuous and effective follow-up of all interested enquiries?

Will they be good negotiators? One test is how they handle their agency appointment negotiations with you. Did they cave in to your requests for a commission fee drop too easily? Such a person will not hold your price up when talking to prospective purchasers who ask, "will the sellers take less"?

Salespeople today are taught to be good negotiators. Certainly that has been one of my obsessions in our training programmes. Purchasers love to test the resolve of sellers on the question of price. If your priority is for a premium price, this will never be achieved if the agent conveys to the buyer the signals that you, the seller, will consider a drop in price.

Also, look closely at the firm behind the agent. That does have impact. The office policies, its local profile and its ability to gain referral leads are all important.

Commitment to service is a trademark of long-term and very successful salespeople. I think that you can recognise this quality not only from testimonials but also from their willingness to guarantee their service. Ask questions about the frequency of the contact that they intend having with you.

You have every right to ask for (and demand!) regular contact with the agent, both through written reports and face-to-face

WHO? Which Agent Will Best Suit Me?

meetings. You'll find that you can always get more information and satisfaction when face to face. Of course, if you live more than an hour's drive away from your property and agent, a weekly meeting may not be practical. However, if I was selling and was even a couple of hours drive away, I'd probably get into the car at least once during the first few weeks and make an appointment to meet face to face with the agent. Living further away means you will have to rely on written reports and telephone conversations.

The frequency of those reports should be established and you must be happy with the time frames agreed on and promises given. If appointing an exclusive agent I'd ask for weekly reports (in writing), phone calls a couple of times a week and "face-to-face" meetings weekly or fortnightly. It's your choice, but if an agent is not willing to commit to a written schedule of contact, then you need to start to question their commitment to your property. Of course, commitments are only as good as the people who make them, so remember to consider the person making the commitment.

It's easy to promise and not deliver – like politicians at election time, some agents promise more than they deliver. We've all heard of sellers who have had lots of service and inspections for the first two weeks then practically nothing until a week or so before the expiry of the agency agreement. You must do all that you can to avoid this situation. It is very poor agency practice and is abhorred by the many professional and responsible real estate agents.

So, ask for a written guarantee of service and a written schedule of that service. Every responsible real estate agency has a week-by-week program of service for controlled listings. Controlled listings are any listing where you have given an agent exclusive rights to sell for a certain period – i.e. multi-list, exclusive, auction and tender (see the chapter on "Selling Methods Explained" for the difference in these methods of marketing). You may even decide that you would rather not have as much contact, but it's your choice not that of the agent.

As I said earlier, commitments are only as good as the people who make them, but if they're in writing, you do have redress. You know the greatest difference between sales people is very often just the level of the service they're willing to offer – and more than just "willing to offer", but "willing to guarantee".

> *When I think of service I'm reminded of an experience I had in Bali where again, with all their wonderful resorts, the difference between each resort is often only the level of their service. While there I celebrated my birthday (21 again!) and the day before my birthday I went to reception to ask the name of a nice restaurant (out of the hotel) and just mentioned in passing that, because it was my birthday the next day, I'd like to go somewhere special. Mentioned only ONCE and just casually in conversation. Next morning, a knock on the door at 9.00am and in came the butler with a BEAUTIFUL birthday cake, iced with "Happy Birthday" (in English, not Indonesian) and four candles! (I thought that the number of candles was very diplomatic!). I thought at first that family or friends had organised this but no! The girl at reception had taken note, said no more to me and then organised her "colleagues" as she called them*

> when I went to thank her. It was so discreet, no big fuss, no "look what I've done", she JUST DID IT! Of course, the hotel has a friend for life – I highly recommend the Sheraton Laguna at Nusa Dua (and get a Lagoon Access room!)

So you should be looking for agents who give you "birthday cake service" above and beyond what you expect.

And now the question of price. Do you appoint your agent on the criteria of who you want to have looking after you OR do you pick the agent just because that person mentions the highest price among all the agents you have spoken to?

Big question! One tendency that has developed in recent years can be summed up in the term "buying your listing". It's based on the theory that all sellers want the premium price (profile 1) and that an agent can obtain any listing merely by promising the highest price – sometimes well over a market premium price!

Be conscious of the danger of this policy, particularly if you are listing with a price. Unfortunately, the first task that the agent will do, once he or she has an exclusive listing, is to prove to the owner why the price needs to be dropped. You, rather than the buyers, becomes the main target of activity of your appointed agent!

I will always appoint the agent in whom I have most confidence and then discuss price with my appointee. Of course, I will have listened to all agents to get a price range (in addition to my own homework) and then chosen a price that fits my profile priorities. The choice of agent should not be made on the price quoted.

An agent's listening skills are so important. If your agent understands your ambitions you will be confident in the advice that they give you.

This becomes so supportive and comforting to you during the selling process itself - a period that can create anxiety for you. That anxiety is increased if you and your agent are not on the same wave length.

At that point you are required to sign an agency agreement. You will have discussed and agreed on the commission rate. This process reveals more about the skills of my prospective agent than any other possible test.

Also, as I have already mentioned, the number of days your agent wants for his or her appointment is a telltale sign of how long they believe your property will take to sell. Will that fit your time profile?

USE THIS CHECKLIST TO SELECT YOUR AGENT

QUALITY OF ADVICE

- Gave clear explanation of selling methods available to you ☐ No choice or explanation was given as to selling methods
- Your CHOICE as to whether or not you want open homes ☐ TOLD that you MUST or must NOT have open homes

PHRASES USED

- "What will suit you?" ☐ "We don't do it that way"
- "What's most important to you – price, speed of sale or privacy?" (They've obviously read this book!) ☐ "There's only one method of selling that works in this area"
- "Where would you like to advertise?" ☐ "We just do general advertising – your property mightn't be advertised"
- "How do you feel about open homes?" ☐ "Open homes don't work!"

HOW DO YOU FEEL

- Confident that he/she understood your situation? ☐ Not confident that the salesperson really knew what you wanted
- Comfortable with the selling suggestions ☐ Uncomfortable with the lack of choice
- Rapport – at ease with the communication with that agent ☐ Ineffectual communication – you're not even on the same wavelength

FINALLY

- Listened carefully to my needs ☐ Told me what I should do

This is probably the agent who will relate to your requirements and help bring the selling process to a satisfactory conclusion.

The choice of this agent will probably lead to a frustrating and unhappy selling process.

Which Agency?

Wouldn't you be disappointed if I didn't talk about the advantage of dealing with a member of a national real estate group? You wouldn't expect anything else!

I know I have spent a considerable amount of time in declaring that "black and white is never right", but there is a limit to this assertion and this is it! There is no denying that there are some very good boutique agencies for whom I have a great respect and who concentrate on a fairly clearly defined geographic area. Then there are some very good large groups with national and international connections. Then there are lots of agencies that fall into neither category.

My "black and white" advice is to choose between the specialist boutique (small but good), or the national group (large but good), with the emphasis – you guessed it – on the latter. That's because you have the best of both worlds, locally owned (as with the boutique) but with all the advantages of access to professional training and a huge network of referrals.

When people move from city to city, state to state or country to country, they long for whatever is familiar – why else would Australians flock to Earls Court in London and Americans to McDonald's ANYWHERE! It's human nature to feel comfortable with the familiar. In Auckland, Perth, Cairns, Christchurch, Albury, Orange and so many other cities, I have heard the comment: "We had someone in the office today because they felt comfortable because they already knew the name Ray White – it reminded them of home." That familiarity attracts buyers when moving to a strange area. It is important for you to have access to "out-of-town" buyers, as so often these are the buyers who will pay that premium price.

In a company such as ours, operating in so many diffuse and varied marketplaces, we all learn from each other all the time. What works in Surfers Paradise (Gold Coast) can be transferred to Double Bay (Sydney), what we've learnt in Gore (South Island, NZ) can be transferred to Hervey Bay (Queensland) and so on. No one is reinventing the wheel. Unfortunately, small agencies are denied this learning process.

Did I mention referrals? If one agency can find you buyers, how many can 600 find? And they don't just come from your own country. The movements between Australia and New Zealand are well documented.

So that's why my commitment and belief lies with a large franchised group – every office locally owned and operated with the advantages of the interaction that comes from multiple offices internationally. It's the best of both worlds.

If one outlet can find you buyers, how many can 600 find?

When it's time to sell your home you'd probably want a local agent to handle the sale.

After all, surely the local agent knows the local area. But think again. If the local agent is also a member of Ray White with our 600 office network, you can count on getting around twelve referrals.

And our experience tells us that the referred buyer is very often the one who'll pay you a premium price for your home. Ray White. Much more than just a local real estate agent.

Ray White.
REAL ESTATE
since 1902

You Will Have to Sign Something!

The catch-cry of "I won't sign anything" is very common but should be qualified to: "I won't sign anything until I fully understand what it is I'm signing." You simply must always be fully aware of what you are signing and that doesn't refer only to real estate – never sign anything you don't understand. You **will** need to sign forms when you list your home with an agent and again when that magic sale becomes reality. New Zealand and each state in Australia differ in their conveyancing laws and requirements – nearly as silly as having different educational requirements! Rather than wade through a myriad of technical information, I'll just discuss the commonalties of all areas. All agents are trained in the legal requirements for their particular area.

One thing is required in every area and that is an authority to sell – called by different names in each area. This form is just what it says. It gives the agent permission to sell your property and without this form it has been suggested that the agent has no right to enter your home. No matter which form of marketing you choose – open, general, exclusive, auctions etc – it will be necessary to sign an authority to sell form. It will probably be the first thing you'll be asked to sign. Without a signature on this form, the agent cannot sell your house. You <u>will</u> need to sign one of these forms if you want to sell, but make absolutely sure that you understand to which type of agreement (open, exclusive etc) you are committing. This form is merely "permission to sell" your property by the agreed selling option.

By the way, if you are under the influence of alcohol, it is most unethical for an agent to get you to sign anything and it's even doubtful if it's legal. I once had an owner who was always "under the weather". With this in mind, when I had a contract to present for his consideration, I arrived on his doorstep at 8.00 in the morning. Big mistake! I think he had barely stopped imbibing from the night before. I dared not risk going away and coming back again, so I just sat there for nearly two hours while his daughter fed him black coffee until we both judged he was sober enough to know what he was doing. So, stay sober or the agent may stay until you are!

There have been several cases reported in the media in which agents supposedly misled owners about the type and the length of agency to which they'd committed themselves. The reporting only ever seemed to find old ladies and the inference was that everyone else could protect themselves. Perhaps it is just that it makes for better television!

However, you MUST at this stage understand the type of agency to which you are committing. You MUST then ask the agent to point out where it shows the number of days that the agreement is current. I really do not believe that agents set out to deceive on purpose, but because there is a lot of legal and real estate jargon on those forms, it can be confusing for anyone.

No matter where your property is, again the same basic rule applies – don't sign anything that you don't fully understand. If you have chosen your agent carefully, you can be guided by them; however, if in any doubt, whatsoever seek independent legal advice. By this time you will have selected a solicitor or conveyancer to act on your behalf and it is part of their duty to explain the process to you.

I strongly recommend, and it is well worth your while, to use a qualified solicitor/conveyancer to look after your interests in this important transaction. A contract may seem simple and straightforward but only a trained person can see any hidden problems. Every real estate agent has stories to tell of apparently simple contracts collapsing because an owner has tried to save a few hundred dollars by endeavouring to do their own conveyancing. Don't let this happen to you. Your solicitor/conveyancer is trained to protect your interests and ensure that all legalities are observed. It is not as easy as you think.

IN SUMMARY:

- Don't sign if you don't understand
- You must sign the relevant forms giving the agent "appointment to act" –i.e. permission to sell
- Make sure the type of marketing stated on this form is as agreed on – i.e. open, exclusive, etc.

- Any changes or additions to any of the listing forms must be initialled by you – i.e. fees, duration of agreement etc.

I have merely given a very brief guide to your rights and responsibilities; your solicitor/conveyancer is the professional to guide you though this process. It would be wrong of me to give specific advice in this area because not only do the laws governing real estate transactions vary from state to state and country to country, but they are also ever changing. Advice given this month could be incorrect next month.

Now Your Property is On the Market, What is Likely to Happen?

You've decided on your selling strategy and selected the agent that you believe will bring that strategy to a successful conclusion – a sale!

During this time there are several ways in which you can assist and several things that you need to understand to make it easier for the agent to sell and easier for the buyer to buy.

You can assist, but not in the same way as I did when we sold our very first home about 40 years ago (we had it built so had absolutely no experience with real estate). After deciding to sell, we spoke to an agent who had been recommended to us and who knew the house. She rang to say she'd be bringing someone through the next morning so I began my preparations, never for one minute thinking that they wouldn't buy our beautiful home. With this in mind, I prepared morning tea. Those were the days of white (always white!) starched tablecloths, dainty napkins, Shelley tea sets, sponge cakes (homemade, of course!) and scones and cream (if you can't remember those days ask your parents or grandparents if that was the case). The agent and buyers arrived, I danced attendance and then sent one of the children to get the neighbours (on both sides) to join the agent, buyers and myself for morning tea. After all, I didn't consider their **not** buying and, of course, they'd like to meet their new neighbours. Full marks to the agent (thank you, Sona!) for not putting a stop to what I now know was a farcical charade – probably a good story to dine out on for years! Of course, they bought it. Did they have a choice? And paid full price (which probably meant we undersold it). Now that is not the right thing to do, and as both owners and buyers are better educated in real estate matters nowadays, I'm sure it is not a situation that would arise. However, the moral of the story is "you must allow people to see themselves living in the home" in order to move the buying process forward.

So the first rule to remember is to absent yourself during inspections, whether it's open home inspection or inspection by appointment. Buyers are always embarrassed if the owner is present and tend to hurry through the inspection – unless, of course, they're FORCED to have morning tea and meet the neighbours! I still can't believe I did that.

Now Your Property is On the Market, What is Likely to Happen?

Agents don't need to talk to sell! One of the concerns owners often express is "but this agent didn't point out to the buyer the great linen cupboard/the 35 power points/the extra laundry space etc. etc". Disappointing as it may be, none of the above will make a buyer decide to buy a house. Some of these things may be the little extra that tips the buyer over the edge, but a good agent recognises that unless a buyer can contact emotionally with a house, no sale will ensue. You know yourself how hard it is to concentrate on how you're feeling when someone is continually chatting in your ear. So the most effective agent won't talk all the time, except to remark occasionally on a positive atmosphere.

"This is such a cheerful room."
"It's be a joy to work in this kitchen."
"What a view!" etc.

The agent knows what the particular interest of each buyer is and can direct their thoughts in that direction. So remember, it's a **negative** for an agent to keep talking all the time.

When an agent makes an appointment with a buyer, whether it's someone they've met from an open home, or who called off a property advertisement, or who enquired from the internet, the first thing he or she will do is to "qualify" them. Sounds terrifying, doesn't it? All it means is that the agent will ask questions about their requirements, about their time frame as to when they will buy and their financial position. This is such a difficult task as so often buyers purchase a property nothing like their selection criteria. A good agent asks questions about the buyer's lifestyle rather than specific questions. Again, it is necessary for the agent to take some licence as to the price range shown to the buyer. Most buyers eventually buy 10-15% above the range they set where they started looking. This is exactly why open homes work so well. This gives buyers the opportunity to look at properties that do not have the features they thought were necessary. And they then fall in love with the house and buy it. An agent may not have shown that house, as it didn't appear to suit their stated needs or finances. The real estate industry abounds with stories of buyers having bought the total opposite of what they SAID they wanted.

So, while some agents talk a lot about their very careful scrutiny, very often they qualify a potential buyer right out of the door! Any agent who tells you that you may not see them very often, as **they** qualify buyers, is not doing their job. They are, in fact, making judgements for these people. Of course, a good agent will always talk to genuine buyers first to ascertain what is most important to them but, from then on, it is necessary to show your property to as many people as may possibly be interested.

You will nearly always be given notice before an agent accompanies a buyer to your property. It is very rare that you cannot be advised that a buyer will be inspecting your home, but sometimes you might not receive as much notice as you'd like. All owners would like at least a day's notice to make sure everything is exactly right, but sometimes you could have as little as 30 minutes to one hour's notice. If a buyer walks in to the office, the agent talks to them, and if he or she believes that your home could be suitable, then that buyer often wants to see the selected properties THEN, not the next day! Please try to be cooperative and understand the situation because, if you make it difficult for the agent (and buyer) to see your home, it sends out negative connotations, rightly or wrongly, to the agent. Only under exceptional circumstances should an agent and buyer arrive totally unannounced, and even then the agent should first come to the door and explain the situation to you before bringing in the buyer in. Actually, in these days of mobile phones, there's no reason why the agent shouldn't at least phone ahead.

If you are not at home, or even if you are, the agent should **always** leave a business card to let you know they have had a buyer through your home. They should call you back at some time that day, or evening, to let you know the buyer's reaction. If they don't call you back, you are within your rights to – and you should – call them to ask for that information.

There is a possibility, if fairly slight, that someone may knock on your door and ask to have a look through your home. **Do not accede to this request.** There are several reasons:

- It could be **anybody** and not necessarily a desirable character.
- If you wanted to sell your house yourself you wouldn't have appointed an agent.
- Give the buyer one of your agent's cards (you should have been given several just for this contingency) and suggest that they call the agent who will organise for them to see your home. If the "door-knocker" is genuine, he or she will do this. If they don't contact the agent, that is more proof that he or she isn't for real.

- Never tell them how much you want for your house, particularly if it's an auction.

Actually, rarely does someone knock on a door these days, but I do find that owners are concerned that it just might happen.

What happens if another agent calls you? For agents to call on another agent's sign is illegal in some states/countries and unprofessional in others. Should an agent call, please don't be swayed by "but we have a buyer". Rather, suggest that in that case they should contact your agent who will "work in with them" – as long as he or she is not already dealing with that buyer. It's just so much easier for you to be dealing with only one agent/agency.

After learning from the success of the sale of our first home, when I went into real estate I found that if I could arrange for a buyer to eat or drink, or both, in a house it helped them make a decision. So you, too, can help. These later inspections are usually by appointment and your agent should tell you if it is a second (or third or fourth!) inspection. You can forgo the starched cloth and Shelley tea set (aren't you pleased about that?) It needs to appear to be spontaneous and **you** won't be there (and neither will your neighbours, unless they're the buyers). If it's a hot day, leave a note to say there's cold juice in the refrigerator and leave glasses and biscuits/cakes on a tray all ready to be taken to the most pleasant part of the house. If you want to be even more in control – and don't we all – take the glasses and food to the table where you'd like them to eat, whether it's inside or out, then just leave a note to tell the agent where you've put the glasses. If it's cold weather, do the same but leave coffee in either the percolator or a thermos. Both scenarios show a thoughtful owner and, strange as it seems, these positive thoughts are transferred to the buyers. Never underestimate the power of subliminal thoughts. By the way, leave a note. Don't just tell the agent because if there's no note, it seems as if you've liaised with the agent. Remember you can't do this with every inspection. It's not appropriate and the agents would all have a weight problem, to say nothing of a time management problem! You should ask your agent if this would be appropriate, taking into account the personality of the buyer involved. Although, on second thought, "just do it", and if the buyer declines the offer, you'll be left with some extra juice or coffee! Now that's as much as you can do to encourage offers and you can rest assured that the agent is trying to get offers. Remember buyers will only buy a house when they can see themselves living in it. I know that some agents in our Sumner office in Christchurch use this encouragement with great results. They call it "doing a Myf" and declare it works wonders!

You can help if you:

- Absent yourself from open homes and all inspections by appointment
- Recognise that agents don't have to talk
- Know how to deal with people who want to buy privately
- Realise the power of improving the quality of second and third inspections

The two things you are entitled to expect during this selling time are inspection and offers, and often it will be more inspections and less offers than you think. It's really hard to imagine that every person who comes through will not want to buy your precious home. But they won't! You'll need to be prepared for the fact that you may not get lots and lots of offers, no matter how hard your agent tries.

Talking about offers, probably the offer that will be most difficult to decide on is the first one. The real estate saying that gets brought out at so many negotiations is "the first offer is the best offer". Talk about black and white!

The first offer MAY be the best offer, or maybe the second or third will be better. Look seriously at EVERY offer and decide on its merits. The trouble is that too many owners dismiss the first offer just because it is the first one. Never do that. Sometimes the real estate agent may even be able to identify the likely buyer from the current people with whom he or she is working. Certainly, they always contact their current buyers as soon as a new property comes on the market.

When you sign all the documents required to sell your property you have, in real estate terms, "listed" your property. Then the other agents in that office need to look at it (in real estate terms, "inspect it") before they can sell it. I've had owners who've complained about "all those agents traipsing through without buyers". It would only be under exceptional circumstances that an agent would bring a buyer to see a property without seeing it first. It would waste the buyer's time as it may be nothing like what they want so, therefore, it wastes your time and that of the agent. So expect the agents to look by themselves first. Sometimes, all the agents from the office come to your property together, and other times they'll inspect individually. I tell you this so you'll understand the process.

Now Your Property is On the Market, What is Likely to Happen?

Talking of first offers, I was talking to a friend who said that she'd spoken to a lady who had called about a property that had a sign on it. She spoke to this lady, who was an active buyer, for some time. The property in question didn't suit and she made an appointment for the next day to show her other properties. Then, that afternoon, my friend listed a property and immediately thought of this lady, as it sounded exactly what she was looking for. She rang her, they looked, and within an hour, she had signed a contract at $5000 less than the asking price. The owners were concerned.

"Why did it sell so quickly?"
"Will someone pay more?"

Both very valid questions but this early offer frightened them. The agent explained that this was a buyer who had been looking for some time etc. The owners were adamant that they would only accept full price at this time, while the buyer was adamant that she would not pay full price, so there was no sale. Of course, you can guess the rest – after four or five weeks the property sold for less than the original offer.

Of course, there are times when first offers aren't the best ones, but all I can ask is that you look at that first offer carefully and ask questions of the agent – you never get into trouble if you ask questions. You only get into trouble when you give the answers.

Ask how long these particular buyers have been looking and whether they have put offers on other properties. Both of those questions tell you about the buyer. If they've been looking for a while, they usually have a good idea of value and are probably keener to buy now (contrary to popular opinion, most buyers don't really enjoy MONTHS of house hunting). If they've put in offers on lots of properties, do they just put in low offers on everything in the hope of getting a bargain? Not many of those around, thank goodness!

The most important question is the one that you have to ask yourself: "Will this allow me to get on with my life and do what I want to do?" If the answer is "yes", then sign!"

Remember:

- Unfortunately, every inspection won't result in an offer
- The agents <u>will</u> need to see your property before they can sell it
- Look carefully at <u>every</u> offer. Do not automatically dismiss an offer because it is the first one

You Never Get a Second Chance...

You never get a second chance to make a first impression. That first impression must be positive when a buyer sees your property.

There are so many little ways in which you can maximise the instant appeal of your home. The effort and expenditure you put into preparing it for sale can be an extremely profitable use of time and money. Emotional decisions are based on sight, sound and smell. Your house must look attractive, the sounds should be unobtrusive and odours should be inoffensive.

The intention here is NOT to make your home presentation too onerous a task - it is quite OK to present a comfortable "lived-in" look. These are just extras for those sellers who so often ask, "What else can I do to improve the presentation?". So often it is embarrassing for agents to suggest improvements and so often while owners ASK, they really want the agent to say "it's perfect!".

So I've noted almost the ultimate recommendations both here and in the chapter "To open or not to open". Choose only the ideas that suit you, your home, your budget! I'm sure that not all of these suggestions would be appropriate for anyone. As always, it's **your** choice.

First of all, go outside, close your eyes (I'm not kidding!) and say: "I'm a buyer seeing this house for the first time." Now open your eyes (or you'll fall over the fence!) and go right through the house from that first moment of arrival and look at it as a potential buyer would see it. Remember, the emotion felt in the first few moments is so important – make sure it's a positive, not a negative, reaction.

EXTERIOR-FRONT GARDEN/FENCE

To maximise the instant appeal of your property, first of all look at the fence and front gate. If they need a touch of paint, do it (make sure it's dry before the first open home!), and fix the hinge on the gate that has stopped it closing for the past two years! Look at the front garden. Mow the lawns a couple of days before so that it looks naturally green by the weekend. Get some flowering plants from the local nursery and use some pine bark or similar ground cover so the weeds will at least stay away until after the sale! It's not hard to create an instant garden. If you find that plants die if you even look at them, employ a handyman/gardener to "pretty" up the garden. You don't have to go to the expense of a landscape architect at this stage – you can use their expertise when you buy your new home.

THE HOUSE

I find that one of the greatest "turnoffs" is rusting gutters. Buyers' eyes are drawn to it like a magnet. "But I'd have to replace the gutters," you might say. But believe me, if you don't replace them, the buyers will take that into account when negotiating and I've heard them say, "And there's those gutters. That's another $5,000 I'd have to pay" – $5000 for gutters! You will **save** money if you repair the gutters.

It's been said that the kitchen and bathroom are the most important areas of a house. I'm not sure about that, but I do know that while they're not the rooms that make someone buy the house, they're often the rooms that make someone **not** buy the house. Does that make sense? So don't let them be a "turnoff". First of all, they must be **clean, clean, clean!** That means no mould in the shower or around the bath, benches free of toothbrushes, cosmetics etc. and replaced with a nice maidenhair fern (they do actually grow quite well in bathrooms) or bowls of soap or similar. Towels should be clean – a good excuse to buy some matching towels, hand towels etc.

The kitchen, too, must be clean, tidy and uncluttered. Keep the benches free of implements as it makes the room look more spacious. A nice big bowl of fruit looks homely and not too arranged.

Then the bedrooms must also be tidy with beds made and clutter removed. The less unnecessary furniture, the bigger the rooms look. The word to describe how the living areas should look is "inviting". Have vases of flowers where you'd expect flowers to be – living areas, entrance hall, and main bedroom. If you have it looking like a florist's shop, it looks too contrived.

If you have a fireplace make sure you make maximum use of its attraction to most people. Buyers are drawn like a magnet to a fire. So if it's a cold day have the fire going, as buyers immediately imagine themselves sitting in front of it – and a good agent will encourage them to do just that! Even if you never light the fires in the bedroom fireplaces, set them and make them look as if you do. Have them set with pinecones, logs etc. I think that fireplaces should be set the whole time the house is on the market, whether it's hot or cold. Fireplaces with vases of flowers or similar in them don't conjure up those same emotions.

It's amazing how a few strategically placed cushions can cover worn furniture – I know they're not buying the furniture, but shabby furniture can suggest an owner who has lost interest or HAS to sell!

We've covered some of the sight, so sound and smell must also be addressed. The best sound is popular classic music. The television is an absolute "no no"; it merely distracts. Rock music is intrusive, as is music with words (songs). Personally, I feel that "mood" music is just too contrived. You can't go wrong with Mozart or a bit of Tchaikovsky. They're both light, inoffensive and are good background. Of course, they must be played very softly; again they mustn't dominate.

Now smells. The most offensive smell is that of animals. The problem is that no matter how house trained our pets are, they often leave a distinct odour of which we are totally unaware –

we've become immune to it. Others walking in will notice it immediately. To remove pet odours, there are two alternatives:

- Remove the pets! That may sound drastic but I've known quite a few people who have put their "house pets" in kennels for the few weeks they've had their house on the market. It's up to you.
- Work very hard with deodorisers but be aware that you don't want your house to have that easily recognisable smell of air-fresheners.

After you've removed the animal smell – one way or another – decide what smell suits your house.

As mentioned in the next chapter on open homes, oil burners are better than incense. The contrived smell of bread or vanilla is probably more appropriate for open homes.

As far as re-painting inside, I probably wouldn't. I've found that sugar soap and elbow grease is often as good as a re-paint. If that sounds like too much hard work, then use commercial cleaners. The basic rule is don't spend too much money but give tender loving care combined with hard work. Then clear the clutter. Have a garage sale – one person's trash is another person's treasure – and you may be amazed at how much money you can make with a morning's work. If you can't bear to be permanently parted from those treasures, then hire one of those "self-storage" modules and fill it with anything that you can live without for a couple of weeks/months. Actually, at the end of the time you can have a garage sale, as by then you will have learnt to live without those possessions! Whichever alternative you use, you'll be amazed at how much tidier and bigger the rooms look.

I suggest that you don't do things like re-carpet, unless it's absolutely essential. Too often this has happened and the colour chosen hasn't suited the buyers. It's a totally different story if you've bought a really, really shabby house and completely renovated it (see chapter on "Renovate or Titivate"). In normal situations the advice is, use elbow grease, titivate smaller things that don't cost a lot of money and put in lots of tender loving care but don't spend heaps of money without getting advice from several real estate agents. They'll be able to tell you what type of property sells in your area.

THE BACK GARDEN

Again an instant garden, as in the front, is effective. Have some outdoor furniture well positioned. You must make people want to live there, so make it look "lived-in" but tidy. If you have a barbecue, put the BBQ tools at the side of it as if you're about to entertain.

Pools must look sparkling with not a hint of algae (no matter the season!) and no sign of leaves. Vacuum the pool in the morning of the open home so it will look as if it's no trouble to keep clean – even if you and I know better! If you use one of those kreepy krawley cleaners (they sure make life easy), remove it before anyone arrives. The pool looks bigger without it.

In Summary, to give the best "first impression":

- Check fence and front gate
- Replace rusted guttering
- Kitchens and bathrooms must sparkle
- Light fireplaces in winter – set it at other times
- Have popular classics playing softly
- "Homely" smells create atmosphere
- Swimming pools must sparkle
- Titivate with "elbow grease", not money

If You are Going to Have a Signboard...

You must realise that no sign will restrict the number of enquiries. If privacy is your top priority (as in seller profiles B and D), then you may make a decision not to have a "For Sale" sign on your property. Whether or not to have a sign is a decision you will probably be asked to make soon after, or at the point of, appointing your agent.

Our research – from a wide range of offices – shows that 22% of the buyers either called directly off the sign or were first attracted by the sign to go to the open home

The buyer who contacts the agent from a sign is very often half qualified – they like the area and they like the exterior, or they wouldn't have called the agent. Very often the sign attracts someone who has always admired the house or area but hadn't intended to buy yet!

One of my favourite stories (it is obvious that I've collected lots during my years in real estate) relates to exactly that scenario. I was the auctioneer and halfway through the auction of a very attractive home an elderly couple arrived, stood at the back of the crowd and immediately started bidding. An auctioneer's nightmare is "what happens if someone bids, is the winning bidder and doesn't know what they're doing". Out of the corner of my mouth, smiling all the while, I said to the agent: "Who are they?" Her quiet reply, "Don't know", didn't help at all, so after I said to her "find out", she went off and then came back and said, "OK". She'd evidently explained that it was a "cash and 10% deposit sale" and was satisfied that all was well. They were the successful bidders and it sold above reserve. As I was still uncomfortable, I said to the agent: "Don't let the under-bidders go." I then went to the couple and congratulated them. Imagine my dismay when they said: "Would it be all right if we saw inside the house?" I again explained that they had bought it and was that OK with them? They assured me that they understood what I said but would still love to see inside. To cut a very long story short, it transpired that they lived three houses away and had been visiting their son in Darwin for the past month or so. They had no idea that the house was for sale until they took their dog for a walk on the morning of the auction. They dashed (probably "tottered" was a closer description of their walking) home to get their cheque book, as they decided it would be perfect for their son and family who would be moving from Darwin in a few months' time. They were a dear old couple and I'm sure their son would be as delighted to live close to them as they were at the thought of his being "just three doors away". I never checked on the thoughts of the daughter-in-law! It's just one of many stories that agents can tell about people who weren't "in the market" at that moment, but seeing a house "they'd always admired", or a street where "they'd always wanted to live" etc, they suddenly showed interest. (NEVER UNDERESTIMATE THE POWER OF A SIGN.)

A photograph on a sign is eye-catching and attractive **but** make sure the photograph is taken of a part of the property that can't be seen. Recently, I saw a "photo-sign" on a property where the photograph displayed was of the front exterior, which was clearly visible from the street. I looked at it and thought: "You're right; that is the property for sale." What a waste of money! Take a photograph of a bright airy room **inside**, or the back of the property or the view – in fact, anything that's attractive and **can't** be seen by the passer-by. By the way, let me give you a tip. When the photographs are being taken (whether for the sign or brochure), put people in some of them – for example, a photo of a pool is more "alive" with children playing in it and a fire is cosier with a couple sitting in front of it. Some real estate photos look **very** dreary! "Photo boards" are worth the extra cost as anything that catches the eye of a potential buyer must be good value. If everyone in your area has a "photo board", you can't afford **not** to have a photograph on your sign, and if no one in your area has such a sign, then imagine how different your property will look with a photograph as well as text.

It is often wise to use a professional photographer, as too often detail is lost in dark or fuzzy photos taken at the wrong time of day. A professional photographer will also make sure that there's not too much sky, grass or road!

Talking of text on a sign, there are a few rules:

- Talk about what **can't** be seen. If it's single storey, if it's brick/timber, don't waste space talking about what can be seen by looking at the property.
- Too much text is messy; keep it brief.
- Use large lettering so that people driving by can get the main message at a glance.
- Make sure the agent's name and phone numbers are prominent so that they can be contacted.
- If you're having open homes, the times should be clear so that it is easy for drivers to see and remember.

SECURITY ISSUE

Then there is also the situation where security may be of concern to the seller. There is the perception within the marketplace that once a "For Sale" sign goes up, the owner will either be inundated with people "knocking on the door" or be robbed and the house vandalised. Actually, this rarely happens. I have only heard of a few people actually approaching the owner. A caring agent will have carefully coached the owner with the dialogue: "Here is my agent's card; you can contact him or her and he or she will be more than happy to talk to you." I'm not sure where the burglary theory came from, because a sign on the property does not necessarily suggest that it is empty. In fact, with established homes, there would be more occupied than empty homes on the market. However, if that is the perception of the marketplace, perception becomes reality.

If you are an elderly person living by yourself and see this as reality and are uncomfortable with a sign, then it is not obligatory, but realise that it may effect the price. **Security can be more important than dollars and cents or speed of the sale.**

While on the question of security, if you live by yourself I suggest that when you put your home on the market you should remind the agent not to state the fact that there is a sole occupant. This applies to when they are at open homes or when he or she brings buyers through on inspections. After my husband died and I sold the family home, I purposely put some of his clothes back in the wardrobe and even found his old "yard" shoes and left them at the back door. I'm quite sure it was not necessary but it was reassuring for me. Sadly, in these days, it is not wise to advertise that you are a woman living alone. It's just common sense.

Remember you have the right to check on the wording and photograph (if used) before the sign goes up. It's your home – be involved at every stage of its marketing.

To Open or Not To Open

Do we really have to open our home for inspection? It is such a bore. Do we have to allow people, some of whom may not be interested, to come into our private world, to pass judgement, to assess suitability and value? Wouldn't it be better if buyers qualified themselves by some other system and only those who were judged to be suitable or qualified were permitted the next stage of visiting and viewing our property?

If your seller profile places least inconvenience and privacy as a substantial priority, then opening your property will not be a policy that appeals to you.

The enduring appeal of open homes is that they are now steadily increasing in popularity with purchasers. Some attendees may be at the very early stages of becoming a committed and active purchaser, and maybe are not as expert or knowledgeable with prices as those that have been looking for some time. The experienced buyers are usually more reliable in their assessment of price and therefore their comments may be more valuable.

If you are determined to achieve a premium price and don't wish to have your home on the market indefinitely, an active open home policy makes sense for one reason – buyers and potential buyers like it.

WHO COMES TO OPEN HOMES?

- Buyers who are in the process of actively searching for a property
- Owners who are deciding whether or not to sell (owners who will probably become buyers)
- Sellers whose property is on the market (and will become buyers!)
- Buyers who will buy in the near future
- The occasional "sticky-beak" and neighbour

Apart from the sticky-beaks, your buyers could come from any one of those categories.

A determined buyer may possibly ring agent who is likely to help – "I need to buy right now. What have you got?" I say, "MAY ring", as more and more of even the most determined buyers are opting for going to multiple open homes. If, however, the buyer does ring, he or she may be taken out and shown five properties, for instance, and be asked, "which one of those five do you want to buy"? That's fine as long as YOUR property is one of the ones selected by the agent AND that purchaser has the capacity to pay your price. With an open home, you are far more likely to get more of these determined buyers choosing to go through your property. More and more buyers are buying a house without ever putting their foot inside a real estate office. Certainly I can remember when most buyers walked into a real estate office and said: "I want to buy a house." Nowadays, buyers find it far more convenient to organise themselves for through newspapers and advertisements for "open homes". It would be incorrect to suggest that someone wanting to buy a house **never** approaches a real estate agent, but it is becoming more infrequent, because of your need to get as many potential buyers as possible through your property.

Then there are the owners who are currently selling and those who may sell, and the buyers who are still looking tentatively. They may be slower to make up their minds and so prefer the anonymity of open homes. They probably don't even realise that they really are buyers, but they are keeping an eye "on the market" through open homes and checking the internet, newspapers, real estate windows and agents' magazines. Something often catches their eye. The chances are they would NEVER phone an agent to see a property. but YOUR property could be in the particular area, or be the particular type of property they want. It's open for inspection. They look and fall in love with it. No fuss.

Suddenly ... it's sold!

Then, there are the other two groups – neighbours and people just looking!

Neighbours – more properties are sold to neighbours than people realise. After all, they know the area and then because they know and presumably like the area, they will act as salespeople for you by telling others about the property.

Sticky-beaks – a necessary evil! I've found "sticky-beaks" often tend to talk a lot and as long as they're telling everyone how great your house is...

It is worth remembering that 26.7% of all our purchasers first saw their new home at an open for inspection. The mathematics certainly supports the effort of opening your home.

OPEN HOMES ARE CONVENIENT FOR:

- **YOU** – Let's face it, selling your home is inconvenient, but at least open homes allow you to organise to a timetable. While you will still get agents bringing some buyers through – buyers they have qualified and met through a number of processes – most inspections will be through "open homes" at a predetermined time.
- **BUYERS** – Buyers find open homes non-threatening and they feel that they can inspect the open homes by themselves. Often buyers are intimidated by some agents and feel pressured. If more buyers will see your home via the medium of open homes, then it is a vehicle that, as

sellers, you can't dismiss. Before open homes were as accepted as they are now, buying a house was a very time-consuming task for the buyer. It was very inconvenient to search papers, look in real estate windows and make appointments with multiple agents who then had to make times with the owners that suited all parties. It took days and weeks. Now it's a case of just selecting from the list of homes open and viewing quite a few homes in one day. If it is convenient for **buyers**, and it is, it is of benefit to **you**.

- **YOUR HOME** – Make sure the agent picks a time when your home will be seen at it's best. If you're in a hot climate and the afternoon sun beats in on the living area, open it late morning, or if it's a "cold" house, pick a time when the sun **does** stream in. If it's facing tidal water, try to time the open homes for high tide, which is more attractive than low tide. This is not trying to present the home other than it is, but first impressions are so important. If a buyer gets a poor first impression, it is very difficult to ever change that impression. Of course, your buyer will want to see the house more than once (well they nearly all do!) so they'll drive past at low tide or realise the property faces a direction where it's cold or hot, but after a first good impression, these often become minor distractions. I remember a disastrous open home I conducted where, because of a lack of forethought on my part, the house was not presented at its best. The house was about 500 metres down the road from a huge sports ground that was not used a lot – apart from Commonwealth Games (once in a lifetime!), athletics carnivals (very occasional and very small), as well as the annual GPS Athletics Carnival. Now, which day in the whole year did I choose? Of course, the day when there were 2000-3000 cheering teenage schoolboys, 1000 enthusiastic and encouraging parents, and at least 3000 screaming girls trying to vocally impress the boys! Well, not only could you not get a park within walking distance, but also **who** would consider a house with that noise in the neighbourhood? Pick a time when a house is at its best – not the half day when it's at its worst. That's when open homes DON'T work!

At least with an "open home" you have time to prepare your home so it looks its very best when most people will see it. If you have one of those homes that looks as if it has just been photographed for *Vogue Decorating* – whether it's 7.00am or 7.00pm or any time between – then skip the next couple of pages. This is for those of us who don't make the bed (complete with matching linen and casually placed cushions!) before breakfast; who don't always have flowers in the main rooms or in the bathroom; and who don't always have artistically arranged bowls of fruit and vegetables on the totally bare kitchen benches! So, if you're like me, read on!

Remember that emotional decisions are based on **sight, sound** and **smell**.

I went into the detail of these areas in the last chapter, explaining how to have your home looking its best – "you never get a second chance." However, there are just a couple of little extras that you can do just for open homes that are not always practical for other times!

The best sound is classical music (soft!) and for open homes, smell is important. Oil burners using subtle oil fragrances are effective, but incense tends to be a "put off". The best smells are those that suggest "home". Bread, vanilla and coffee all work a treat. Vanilla beans in a saucer of water, and with the oven on low, will give a great smell of cooking. You can either roast coffee beans in the oven (and then turn off the oven) or have a percolator brewing. I think the coffee-bean trick gives a better aroma. Be careful of the bread idea. The theory is, soak a loaf of bread in milk and then re-bake it in the oven. Gives off this good smell of bread baking. I remember one of our salespeople suggested this to a young couple who were selling their house. The husband was in charge of the "bread thing" and duly did as had been suggested. What the agent hadn't told him was at what temperature the oven should be set, so what did he do? Of course, he set it on high, very high! The owners departed about 20 minutes before the open home and the agent opened up and thought there was a slightly burnt smell but decided it was just burnt toast (sure was!) He was standing at the front door, and just as the first people arrived, the smoke alarms suddenly went off. They all rushed to the kitchen to see lots of smoke – fortunately, no flames! Every one of those senses we spoke about had been violated – sight (lots of smoke), smell (burnt bread) and sound (the piercing noise of the smoke alarms). It wasn't a good start. The agent, assisted by the open home visitors, opened windows and "fanned" madly. He then found the air-freshener and generously sprayed it everywhere, with the result that the house smelt like a motel bathroom rather than freshly baked bread! The moral is, don't put the men in charge of the "smells"!

Some agents don't like open homes. There are different reasons for this. Perhaps they believe your home doesn't have the appeal to bring potential buyers – that fundamentally it's a waste of time. There could be a number of like properties for sale in the immediate vicinity. These properties may be slow moving. Why suggest the seller experience the inconvenience of an open home if the agent has no expectation of promising activity?

Then again, an agent might not like opening homes as his operating policy. An open home takes time. Maybe he or she would prefer to be doing something else.

A technique used by some unprofessional agents is to frighten sellers by saying "criminals come to open homes". But fears of security are easily fanned and have little basis in fact. Nowhere in the English-speaking world is this a problem, but the technique often works. Sellers 'freeze", miss out on the opportunity of more potential buyers seeing their property and rely solely on the agent deciding whether or not to show that property to buyers that the agent may identify.

My advice is to see through that claim for what it really is – a poor excuse to get out of the responsibility to seek the premium price for their sellers, if that is the seller profile.

Your typical 'open for inspection' criminal?

Some real estate agents will do anything to get their own way. They don't want to make the commitment to market your home properly.

How do they get out of opening your home for inspection?

Simple. They worry you by saying criminals may attend an open for inspection. Yet more than 26% of all Ray White buyers first saw their home at an organised open for inspection.

These are your typical criminals?

Of course, your home's security has always been one of our highest priorities.

More than adequate staff are on hand to insist that all buyers provide details as a requirement of entry. No details no entry.

Any agent can sit back and hope for the telephone to ring. Ask your agent whether they are prepared to do the hard yards.

When you think of it, they're not keeping burglars out, they're keeping the right buyer out!

Now that really is criminal.

Ray White
REAL ESTATE

HOW LONG TO HAVE YOUR HOME OPENED?

As to how long and how often you should have your home opened, your agent should have experience and know what works best in your area. After much trial and error over the years, we have found that 30 minutes is sufficient in most areas. By shortening to this time, you are more likely to have more than one group of buyers there at a time and so promote competition and action because they realise that others could also be interested in the property.

How often to open your home depends on your area. It seems that the closer to the centre of the city/town, the more popular open homes will be. Certainly, I'd think you'd be entitled to ask for one open home per weekend for an auction and one every second weekend for an exclusive agency. Midweek open homes work in some areas and are just great to encourage "second" looks. Even if only two groups of people come through, it's more than you'd get if the agent sat in the office and waited from someone to walk in and enquire about your property.

The easier you make it for buyers to see through your home, the longer they are likely to take to view it and the longer they are in the property, the more likely they are to buy it.

By all means dismiss opening your home if it does not suit your seller profile, but never on the argument that it doesn't suit your agent. Remember, buyers like open homes - 26.7% of our buyers came from open homes - and if it brings more buyers then it's better for you.

Closed for inspection.
(Closed to buyers)

Open for inspection.
(Open to buyers)

The property on the left has an uncommitted agent who can't be bothered opening his homes for inspection.

He uses excuses like, 'Don't open, criminals will come,' as a smokescreen to confuse his clients.

The property on the right has a Ray White agent, committed to getting the premium price for his vendor.

Ray White agents are 'active' agents who open their owners' homes for short, tightly-managed inspection periods.

In our experience, the more interest shown in a property, the greater the probability of achieving its premium price.

Did you know, for example, that more than 26% of all buyers first saw their home during an Open For Inspection?

That's 26% more buyers than uncommitted agents ever get to see.

Ray White.
REAL ESTATE

The Issue of Advertising?

Does advertising work?

Have you ever realised the extent that real estate advertising encompasses?

From free, throw-over-the-fence, black and white "papers", to high-quality, glossy magazines offering excellent colour reproduction – it comes in all shades. From ads promoting bargains to properties that represent exclusivity. Sometimes the individual property is disguised and at other times, the address of the property is featured. The value of advertising for selling property has been proven over the years, is still relevant today and remains a key question for you when selling.

Seller profiles that seek premium price success and/or speed of transaction invariably are interested in discussing an advertising programme for their property.

This real estate agent says advertising doesn't work.

This is his pantry.

Can you believe those real estate agents who won't advertise your home when you want to sell? They say they don't believe advertising works, yet they are the very same people who buy advertised products.

They wake up in advertised beds, use advertised toiletries, and wear designer-label clothes which, of course, are advertised.

After drinking their advertised coffee and breakfasting on advertised cereal or toast (made in advertised toasters), they drive to work in advertised cars. Then they have the gall to say that people selling their homes shouldn't advertise the fact.

Ray White knows how to advertise your home. And we have advertising that works for all budgets. With annual sales of over $10 billion, try telling Ray White customers advertising doesn't pay.

Ray White
REAL ESTATE

The Issue of Advertising?

And the options are generally extensive.

Perhaps the first question is – do we pay for the advertising or do our agents? It is not uncommon for agents to offer an advertising programme at their risk. In other situations, sellers pay a separate advertising budget, independent of whether the property is sold or not.

As usual, it all depends on expectations and the particular circumstances relating to the location and type of property to be offered.

At the end of the day, it is all a matter of risk. If the owner pays, then what percentage of risk is it? Say an advertising budget of 1.5% of the property's rough value of $200,000 means a budget of $3,000. So the vendor risks $3,000 to protect the $200,000. If the agent was to pay for it, and the property did not sell (for any of many reasons, including a seller's change of mind), that is a huge percentage of the likely gross commission that would relate to a successful sale. The commission on a $200,000 house could vary from $4000 to $8000 (according to state/country). For the agent to risk $3,000 (the advertising budget) to protect $4000 to $8000 is a different decision.

It all becomes complex. Some offices charge a higher commission than elsewhere, but will carry an advertising component. Other offices charge a reduced commission but receive the prepayment for an agreed advertising budget. Other agents may charge a commission in between those two rates but will carry the advertising until sold.

It's all a matter of what strategy suits you best. The key is the quality of communication between you and your chosen agent.

A lot also depends on how your competition (other properties for sale) is presented to the market. Buyers like as few different publications as possible to gain information about availability. It's common sense.

Some agents are able to put together a budget they can carry until the property is sold.

Other considerations include the question: "Will the home be open for inspection?" If so, then the ad needs to be sufficiently prominent to attract those buyers wanting to inspect home opens.

Some agents prefer not to advertise the specific property but to place teaser ads promoting a property that will draw enquiry. And from that they will seek to redirect that enquiry to other listings that agency has.

All this should be discussed at the time of listing. The proposed place of each prospective ad should be detailed and form part of the agency appointment discussion. Once again, sellers should seek to know how buyers for their style of property in their general location prefer to source their information. It all comes back to identifying how to locate the anticipated buyer – "where will my buyer come from"? Make sure this question is uppermost in your agent's mind when discussing an advertising programme.

So a decision will be made. Certainly it is an attractive concept for your agent to be taking the risk – but, in your particular circumstances and keeping in mind your priorities, will that curtail your property's exposure and ability to attract the right buyer/buyers? **Will the marketing of your property be jeopardised because the scope of advertising has been restricted to a level that the agent can justify?** Will the saving now of a few hundred or even thousand dollars result in a lesser price because the number and quality of buyers have been restricted because of insufficient advertising?

I've seen cases when the advertising budget actually exceeded the commission. Let me tell you about such a case.

> We had a **mountain** to sell! It was a long, long way from anywhere, absolutely no facilities at all, useless for anything except trail-bike riding, solitude or just being able to tell your friends that you owned a mountain! It was also **very** well priced – not that we had any other mountains to do a comparative market analysis – and the owner had been trying to sell it for a long time. I talked of the value, and in this case, the absolute necessity to advertise. I think other agencies had been waiting for someone to walk into the office and ask if they had a mountain for sale! The owners became so enthusiastic about the opportunities advertising would offer that they decided on a large ad in the Courier-Mail (Brisbane). This one ad represented approx 3% of the value of the property but they insisted that "a mountain required an impressive ad!" Who was I to argue as I wasn't experienced in selling remote and unusable mountains,

> *but it did go against my belief that the size often reflected the price of the property in the minds of buyers. You can guess the results – from the moment the ad appeared in the paper the phone rang hot. After giving directions to dozens of enquirers we sold it that morning for full asking price, to a buyer, who after hearing of the interest, didn't even wait to see it. He bought it sight unseen. I'm sure a smaller ad would not have had anything like that response. The ad could not be missed which was important as I'm sure not one of the enquirers opened the Courier-Mail that morning to see what "mountains were for sale"!*

The fact that the advertising was more than the commission was irrelevant to the owner who achieved the desired sale with that investment in the advertising.

Where is the most favoured medium that likely purchasers will refer to? The choices are metropolitan, local, regional and specialised real estate magazines. The specialist magazines, often published by real estate agents, are economical and effective as they have a longer "shelf" life and good-quality reproduction. People tend to read black and white publications and then discard them but there is a general reluctance to throw away colour and glossy publications.

But above all where will YOUR property fit? Your major consideration must be: "Where will my buyer come from? How can I make sure that person is aware of my property?"

Where a property is of interest to a specific clientele then imagination should be used in selecting the advertising medium.

The Issue of Advertising?

Two examples: One of our Christchurch offices had an award-winning garden (with average home attached) for sale. The first ads in the *Christchurch Press* bought limited enquiry but no sale. The agent then decided that the buyer would be someone who would buy it for the garden and so arranged for an ad in the gardening magazine that had done an article on the garden six months before. Sure enough it worked; she sold it to an avid gardener from Invercargill who, on seeing the ad in the magazine, decided that it was time to retire to a warmer climate! Well Christchurch is warmer than Invercargill! Again, a case of "Where will I find my buyer"?

Then there was the example of the dog-boarding kennels for sale. They were advertised in the property section, the businesses for sale, but the buyer came from the ad in a dog-breeding magazine.

These things seem so obvious once they happen but I find that very often neither agents nor owners keep asking the question: "Where will the buyer for this property come from?"

Again, do your homework! Look at the properties advertised. Where would yours fit?

How much to spend? What size ad do I need? A useful check seems to be:

- What size would be too large and just a waste of money
- What size would be too small to be effective

Then select about halfway! Of course, if you have a MOUNTAIN to sell....

So who gets the benefit from advertising? Sellers, buyers or the agent?

The answer: ALL THREE!

Of course, the <u>agent</u> gets a benefit in that he or she has more buyers to encourage to see that property.

The <u>buyer</u> – it often helps them make a decision and "get going". Many "passive" buyers have gone from "maybe soon we'll get organised" to buying a property in one weekend as the result of seeing an ad for a property that appealed to them.

The <u>seller</u> – if premium price and speed of sale are important then they have put themselves in the best position possible.

Now let's look at more detailed information.

The rest of this chapter is for those who would like to be more involved in the process of planning the content and exactly where the ads should be placed. This a personal choice – some owners want to be involved while other say "just show me the finished ad".

The agent may choose one of several methods of planning your advertising schedule. The first involves the agent preparing a total programme of all advertising and expenses. They may present just one recommended schedule or give you a choice of two or three different programmes. The schedule will list such costs as searches, signs, brochures and, of course, media advertising. This schedule should detail the size of the ad, which paper it will be in and the frequency and dates of these insertions. Make sure you ask to see the actual size of the ad because really

8cm x 2col, for example, doesn't give you much idea of what it will look like. You are at liberty to ask for any variation on these schedules but do be guided by your agent.

Some agents prefer to build the programme with the owner. You will look at different size ads, judge the worth of different papers and decide on the frequency. There is little difference in either method – usually just the agent's modus operandi.

When planning your advertising schedule there are three important points to consider:

- Where
- Size
- Content

WHERE DO YOU ADVERTISE?

For the majority of your advertising, use the paper/papers where most properties in your area and your price bracket are advertised. You may do some supplementary advertising in more exotic publications but basically the papers most likely to produce results are the ones where there are lots of similar properties. Buyers always look at the papers that give most choice.

The choices are:

- **Metropolitan** – the main paper of capital or large cities eg *Melbourne* Age, *Sydney Morning Herald*, *Brisbane*

Courier-Mail, West Australian, Adelaide Advertiser, New Zealand Herald, Hobart Mercury, etc.

- **Regional** – the main paper of regional cities eg *Cairns Post, Christchurch Press, Townsville Bulletin* etc.
- **Suburban** – usually free papers published in districts of larger cities and often only read by those within the local area where certainly a percentage of buyers come from. Their circulation is not on as greater a scale as the metropolitan or regional papers.
- **Real Estate dominated publications** – really didn't know what to call this type of publication. They are usually formatted in magazine style, are top-quality publications, in full colour, and are often the dominant source of real estate in the area. The areas where these are found are usually inner city and/or upper end of the market eg *Wentworth Courier, Brisbane News* etc.
- **Real Estate Company Magazines** – these are produced by individual real estate companies and are usually full colour. They are distributed through the individual agencies and get to the "target market" more than some other publications. They are totally real estate-oriented and of interest to those people buying or selling (or thinking of it).

When selecting your advertising medium, your major consideration must be: "Where will my buyer come from? How can I make sure that person is aware of my property?" The newspaper is still the primary choice of buyers when looking for property. I say "still" as certainly more and more people use the internet – but not the majority yet! The other point is that they

The Issue of Advertising?

will tend to look in the major metropolitan or regional paper unless, as in some "inner" suburbs, there is a large predominantly real estate paper eg. *Wentworth Courier* etc.

It is sometimes tempting to say: "I'll advertise my property in an interstate paper in the hope of getting an interstate buyer." (Everyone believes that the mythical interstate buyer may not know value and will pay a premium!) Don't do it. It's a waste of money unless you have an absolutely unique property that may attract an emotional buyer who had no intention of purchasing – for example, "an eco-lodge in the middle of the rainforest", a "secluded island" or similar. Remember the average buyer will always check out the appropriate metropolitan or local paper. If you were moving from Melbourne to Brisbane would you look in *The Age* to see what was available in Brisbane?

Try different papers and industry or related magazines but remember, always include the paper with the largest real estate readership for your area.

SIZE

This is quite a dilemma because you don't want to "waste" money yet you don't want to miss out on a buyer. As mentioned earlier, strike a balance between a "waste of money" and "insignificance".

There is no law that says every ad has to be the same size every time you advertise. Always start with the larger-size ads so that you don't waste that valuable early selling period. You can reduce the size later if that better suits your budget. Be advised by your agent.

My experience has shown that advertisements with a photograph are well worth the outlay. Where colour photographs are available, again they're worth the extra outlay. If you were a buyer looking for a home, which part of the paper would catch your eye – colour photographs or little three/four-line classifieds? Let's blame television; we've become accustomed to photographs and colour.

You should always ask to have final approval of the photo and text used.

When I auctioned my house in Melbourne (the pink one!), after the first week of advertising, the agent and I thought we weren't getting the "right" buyers. So we put pointer ads under different suburbs that referred back to the main ad. This probably only makes sense to anyone who is familiar with the real estate advertising layout in *The Age*. Suffice to say that during the campaign I increased what I'd first decided to spend in order to increase the range of buyers. It worked!

Will buyers find your home?

Bet they will now!

If your home is one of those advertised on the left, you may have an agent who won't make every effort to get you a premium price. This agent will probably tell you display advertising doesn't work.

He'll try to convince you that he'll get enough people to inspect your home, not only without proper exposure, but without opening it for inspection either.

He's an uncommitted agent.

If your home is advertised on the right, you have an active agent who wants to get you a premium price.

This agent is marketing your home effectively and will open it for inspection as well. Who'll get the best possible price?

Bet you it's the active agent: Ray White. After all, we have the numbers to prove it: 60,000 Australians were sold on Ray White last year.

We must be doing something right.

CONTENT

You've seen those ads that, unless you have a glossary of real estate terms, are totally confusing:

"3 b.r. ens, 2 b.i., s.l.u.g., i.g. pool, o.f.p, w.i. pantry, w.o.&h.p."

Maybe a slight exaggeration! What buyer will call on that ad? Only a real estate agent could decipher it.

(For your information, I'll decode it for you ... Three bedrooms, ensuite, 2 built-in robes, single lock-up garage, in-ground pool, open fireplace, walk-in pantry, wall oven and hot plates).

Not only must the ad get the phone to ring, but its primary purpose is "to sell your house". So the ad for your property must sell the benefits of your home specifically.

Different buyers respond to different emotions and it's not possible to write an ad that appeals to all buyers. It makes good sense to change the text of the advertisement in order to attract as many potential buyers as possible. Ask your agent if this is possible – it is and you have every right to ask for this service.

Just a few words about what information should go in the ads. Again be guided by the agent, as they know best what information is likely to get potential buyer enquiry. Don't give too much information. If you tell **everything** there's no need for them to view the property and no chance of their buying it.

The Issue of Advertising?

So many real estate ads contain gross exaggerations – haven't you seen "city glimpses", which probably means that if the neighbours cut down two large trees **and** you then stood on a step ladder or climbed on the roof **and** it was a clear night, you'd see some city lights! My daughter once went to an open home that said "short stroll to zyx school". When she checked she found that it probably would have taken even Cathy Freeman quite a time! It is just so wrong and, believe me, it won't endear buyers to your home if the agent has **over-sold** the property. You are better to **under-sell** and **over-deliver**. Of course, the ad has to be good enough to get the buyer to enquire or attend but keep something as a surprise. No one will buy a property if their dominant thought, on viewing it, is "by the ad, I thought it would be better than this". Before someone will buy a property they need to be **excited**, not **disappointed**, so resist the temptation to tell **everything**!

Every ad is a mixture of benefits and features - the features are the facts (fireplace) while the benefits show the emotion (warm in winter). **Only** features makes a boring ad, and **only** benefits lack credibility. I remember an advertising programme one of our offices did, with great trepidation, for the state manager of a huge advertising company. They were delighted when he insisted on writing the ad but a little concerned when he said he wanted the pictorial section of the paper but with no picture, just text. Who was a real estate agent to question someone whose job was advertising? The ad came out and it was beautifully written and went something like: "My wife and children are devastated at having to leave this haven (I remember the "haven" bit!). What will we miss – we'll miss the kookaburras in the mornings...." And so it continued in that vein. Nothing about the house – was it a house, no one could tell! Such was the emotion expressed, you could hear the violins playing and you needed to get out the tissues. I rang the agent on the Monday to say: "What a "beautiful ad; how many calls did you get?" Her answer: "Every agent in the area called to say what a wonderful ad and **not one buyer!**" The trouble was, no one could understand what it was all about. It was **all** benefits and **no** features. The postscript was, the next week there was an excellent photo (of the pool actually) with text that still promised benefits but also gave factual information, which the agent and advertising executive brainstormed together. Lots of calls – this time from buyers!

Personally, I think that the best idea is to decide with the agent **what** features/benefits should be included in the ad, allow the agent to compose the ad and then approve it before printing. You may prefer a different approach – your choice – but remember the above story!

Also, remember that you don't have to use the same text for **every** ad. There is sometimes an extra charge (by the papers) if you change the photo, but rarely if you only change the text.

For the best chance of success:

- Don't tell everything in the ad
- Under-sell, don't over-sell
- Mix facts and emotion i.e. features and benefits
- Be involved with the content of the ad
- Approve the copy (but be guided by your agent)
- Change the text if it's not working

Turning an Offer into a Sale!

How do you turn an unacceptable offer into an acceptable sale? You negotiate. You will need to accept that negotiating is an integral part of every sale. It will be a rare situation in which an original offer is accepted unconditionally. Too many agents and owners, I guess, believe that the only area of negotiation is price. As in sellers' profiles B, D, E & F, price was not the primary motivation of those owners; lots of other factors came into play.

I would love to be able to tell you that every buyer who inspects your property will make an offer, but it just doesn't happen like that. Certainly, when my own properties have been for sale, I just couldn't understand why every person who went through my much-loved home didn't fall in love with it – but they didn't! Guess it's just the same way that we find it hard to realise that not everyone sees our children and grandchildren as the perfect beings that we believe and know they are!

In N.SW, every owner has to have a contract of sale prepared by a solicitor or licenced conveyancer before any property can be advertised or promoted. Very often (no black or white here!) in NSW, offers are often not actually written on the contract until the agent thinks that it will be accepted. Therefore earlier offers may be verbal. If the buyer wishes to change other parts of the contract or add or change special conditions, in NSW this can only be authorised by your solicitor. Just signing the contract does not denote finalisation as it is not binding until "exchange" takes place – i.e. both solicitors have seen and "exchanged" completed contracts. It is in your and the agent's interest to ensure that exchange takes place as quickly as possible. There would appear to be less negotiating on minor points here than in other areas. It is a more complicated system of conveyancing and probably NSW readers should just skip the rest of this chapter – unless, of course, you are planning to move interstate or to New Zealand.

When an agent has an offer from a serious buyer nearly always that offer will be presented to you on a written contract of sale. This contract will detail the full names of the owners and the buyers, any easements etc. as discussed with you when listing, and inclusions and exclusions. Then there will be the parts you'll be really interested in, the deposit, how much they're offering and under what conditions those offers are being made, along with the preferred settlement date. Apart from the easements etc, every one of those items is negotiable.

But the most common negotiating points will nearly always be in the price. I know that you'd like me to be able to say that there is a mathematical formula that applies to adjusting the price when negotiating, but it just isn't as easy as that. There are, however, questions that you need to ask your agent:

Have you contacted all the other buyers who have viewed my property?
Are any of them interested in buying it?
How much would they pay?

Then look at the market information that your agent has given you and re-consider how much you need to "allow you to get on with your life". You may decide not to divulge that "bottom" price immediately, but perhaps meet the buyers halfway. Continued negotiation often involves the agent going from seller to buyer again and again, until both parties have reached a figure with which they are satisfied. Without doubt, this part of selling is emotional and concerning – after all, it's real money you're talking about, not just figures on a piece of paper.

If your priority of desires puts premium price as your top consideration then, of course, you will take more risks with your negotiating. You will not make as great a change to the price in order to "tempt" the buyer to increase the offer considerably but, at the same time, you'll recognise the risk of the buyer "walking".

If speed/privacy rank above that price, then you may wish to only make adjustments that will be closer to the buyer's offer **or** you may even accept that offer if it "allows you to get on with your life".

Then there's inclusions and exclusions. When you first listed your house the agent would have discussed what traditionally stays, any extras you may be leaving and anything extra you may be taking.

Traditionally what stays are:

- Curtains
- Blinds
- Stove
- Dishwasher (unless mobile)
- Light fittings
- Plants/shrubs etc.

Curtains – if they match the bedspread, either leave the bedspread or change the curtains before any potential buyers have been through your property. I have seen so many contracts fail to materialise because the curtains weren't changed to the buyer's expectations or were just not replaced.

Light fittings – as above. Change now!

Plants etc – if the plants are <u>in</u> the garden they must stay. I once sold a house and one of my daughters, who was supervising the move, dug up and gave all my roses and azaleas to her friends. She was very pleased with this generous gesture, but I had to quickly organise a nursery with fully grown plants to replace those taken – and you know how expensive that is!

So that leaves the "extras" you may wish or be willing to leave. When I say negotiating really starts as soon as you list, it's these extras to which I refer.

Turning an Offer into a Sale!

Let me give an example – A friend in Auckland was selling the large family home, complete with multiple living areas and a full-sized billiard table, and moving to a gorgeous little terrace house in Ponsonby. Now she had absolutely no use for the billiard table. Have you ever tried to fit a full-sized billiard table into a terrace house, and besides that, she couldn't even play billiards! When she told the agent at the point of listing, that she'd leave the billiard table he wisely suggested that she use it as an extra negotiating tool. Had it been included in the original list of "chattels" it would have made not one cent's difference to the buyer's offer. By waiting until well into the negotiating the agent was able to get another $3000 "if the owner will leave the billiard table"! Of course, this would only apply to "big-ticket" items. One can hardly say: "I'll leave the pot plants if you pay another $1,000!" Of course, you are acting on the assumption that the new buyers will WANT that extra article.

I remember one particular auction I attended as an onlooker, where the "garden" consisted of a fair amount of green concrete with numerous "statues" scattered on the small front lawn. When the auctioneer asked whether there were any questions, someone asked if the statues stayed. The auctioneer commented that they could be included in the contract if it was so desired. Everyone laughed at the attendee's reply: "No way, I just wanted to make sure they **didn't** stay!" So be prepared to dispose of those extras in another way if necessary.

IS THERE A DEPOSIT?

Ten per cent of the offered price is the maximum deposit that should be offered. Sometimes the deposit may be less and sometimes it may be paid in installments – i.e. $X now with $Y to be paid by a certain time and date. Always ask the reason if insufficient (less than 10%) deposit has been paid. There may be a perfectly acceptable reason and, if so, you have every right to know. The deposit is really proof of intent to buy and often the larger the deposit, the greater the intent. Should the buyer default on the contract for a reason not covered by the contract, then that deposit is forfeited by the buyer and becomes your property, after the commission earned by the salesperson has been deducted. So you must have a deposit considerably more than just the commission. I do not have a lot of time for agents who only take a deposit sufficient to cover the commission as I consider that they are putting their interest before that of their client (the owner). So the amount of the deposit must be of interest to you. The deposit is held in the trust account of the real estate agency, is completely safe, earns no interest and can only be released on settlement – except for those states where a special release is allowed.

WHAT IS THE SETTLEMENT DATE?

A satisfactory settlement date can be worth thousands of dollars to you. It may mean you only move once, or you don't have to rent for a month or two, or the children don't have to change school at an inconvenient time. Don't change the settlement date for a "minor" reason without asking the agent if the buyer had a special reason for selecting that date. For a contract to be successfully negotiated, both sides must be satisfied.

SPECIAL CONDITIONS

The most common special conditions relate to finance, pest control and building inspection.

There can be several variations on "subject to finance", although more and more contracts are now "cash". That doesn't mean that they have all the money sitting in the bank. It just means that they are pre-approved to a certain limit. There are so many financial brokers working in the marketplace and I know that quite a large proportion of the loans processed through Ray White Financial Services are pre-approved often before the buyer has even started to look.

A "subject to finance" can refer to two different circumstances.

- The buyer has seen a mortgage broker/bank and had finance approved to a certain amount but that approval may be subject to the property standing up to valuation.
- The buyer has not organised the finance at all. In this case you have every right to ask questions about the amount they are to borrow and the chances of their getting that approval. A conscientious agent would have made those inquiries when qualifying the buyer.

In either case, there is now no need for long "subject to finance" clauses as, nearly always, approval can be granted within seven to 14 days.

Pest and Building inspections – very often the contract presented to you will be subject to pest and/or building inspections. While it is wise for you to get BOTH before putting your house on the market, and have those inspections available for the buyer to peruse, don't take it as a personal insult should the buyer want their own inspections. It's not that they don't trust you, it's just that they want another opinion!

DON'T SHOOT THE MESSENGER

The role of the agent is as a go-between between potential buyers and yourself. A good agent acts as a conduit for information between all interested and involved parties – a good agent is a "messenger". Sometimes that messenger has to relay information that may not please you. The Real Estate Institute states that an agent cannot decide whether or not to relay an offer to the owner, but it is their duty to acquaint an owner **whenever** there is an offer, no matter the amount of that offer. When an offer lower than the owner is expecting is relayed, there is often only one person on whom they can vent their anger – the **agent**! Please don't shoot the messenger! It is unethical not to let you know what the market is saying. So often people have said to me: "Don't even tell me if someone says less than $XXX." My answer always was: "Yes I will and I must." If you understand that it is **not** the agent making that offer, you will be more understanding. Believe me, agents dislike those "cheeky" offers as much as you do – because they know the chances are you'll vent your anger on them!

When an agent brings a contract to you, peruse it carefully and ask as many questions as you need so that you understand EXACTLY what you are signing. If an agent cannot answer your questions, at that time, then wait until he or she can. You don't have to accept the first price offered unless you are very happy with it. Negotiation is going backwards and forwards from buyer to owner and then backwards and forwards again and again until a satisfactory agreement is reached. Don't give up. It is often much easier to work with the buyers that the agent has identified than to go out and find another buyer – who might offer even less! And then you start the process all over again.

As mentioned earlier in the chapter, before signing a contract you should ask if the agent, or one of his colleagues, has any other interested buyers. I am quite sure that every professional agent would have canvassed any other buyer who had shown interest to ascertain whether or not they, too, wished to make an offer. But ask just in case!

A FEW MORE TIPS

- **Listen to what the "market" (i.e. buyers) say about your property.** The chances are your property will eventually sell for a figure round about what the buyers are talking.

- **Don't sign anything if you don't understand what is implied with every term and condition stated.** Don't be embarrassed to ask questions. It takes agents a lot of training before they understand these agreements – many of them very complicated – so you can't be expected to understand them without question.

- **Remember if you change any part of the contract/agreement, you negate every part of that agreement.** The most common illness suffered by a vast majority of buyers is known as "buyers' remorse". As soon as they've signed they have panic attacks – "Have we done the right thing?" etc. Now if there's a "cooling-off period", it is up to the agent to nurse the buyers through that period. Some states have a "cooling-off" period, which can vary from three to five working days, and the buyer has the ability to change their mind during that time. There are certain circumstances which negate this privilege – ask your agent to explain to you if there is a cooling-off period in your area and what are the terms of that period. If, however, there is no "cooling off", which is even scarier for the buyer, and you change even the settlement date, the contract is no longer binding until that buyer initials and so acknowledges and accepts that change. I've seen owners decide to change the price offered by just $1000, so allowing the buyer to have second thoughts (and they sometimes do!). You cannot go back and say "I'll now take the first offer of $..." because it's too late. So, the moral is, don't change without realising the consequences of that change. If you're talking considerable amounts of money, of course, you'll change (and initial) until you're satisfied.

- **Ask yourself: "Will this agreement with this price and these conditions, allow me to get on with my life."** If your answer is "yes", then sign it and get on with your life! Personally I think that's really the crux of the matter; if you're too greedy you sometimes end up with less. Every agent has stories of owners who turned down a certain amount and ended up accepting less later on in the selling process.

An agent may do everything possible to sell your home for you. They may advertise and faithfully follow every lead and still not get you the result you want. Certainly question the service the agent gives if it is not satisfactory, but remember they cannot manufacture buyers or make them pay what you'd like.

In summary:

- Look carefully at every offer
- Check deposit, inclusions, exclusions, finance
- Don't change the contract just for the "sake of changing"
- If the offer lets you do what you want to do and "get on with your life", shouldn't you accept it?

Special Circumstances

There are certain unique situations that have not been covered in the previous chapters. Rather than just try to include them where they didn't really fit, I've made them seem important by giving them their own section.

Actually, each situation is important to the minority groups of sellers involved.

How do you best dispose of bequeathed property – Aunt Mary has left her house....

What are the ramifications if I buy before I sell – that's assuming that some of the funds from the first sale are required to finance the second sale.

In fact, should I sell at all or retain and rent and then buy another property.

The perennial question, do you extend or buy? The family home is too small but do you add on or do you sell and buy a larger home?

If you buy a house to renovate how can you make it into a successful (read profitable!) venture.

Unfortunately, in these times, the alternative methods of disposing of the joint home in the case of a divorce/separation must be addressed.

Then no one can ignore the value of the internet as a selling tool.

Then just in case you thought that auctions were an inflexible selling method, I've included stories to refute that theory.

In all the above cases I've assumed that you are selling your own home where you are living. A lot of this also applies to landlords selling their investments but there are specific differences that I've then addressed.

These are all-important situations where some of you may find yourselves – not in all of them, I'd hope!

So Great-Aunty Mary Has Left You Her House

But she's also left it to your five cousins! And you haven't seen any of them for years!

The above screams "nightmare" to every real estate agent unless you can come to an amicable arrangement between yourselves before calling in an agent. For example, who will decide on:

- Method of selling.
- Advertising – if any/size etc.
- Acceptable price.

Whether you decide to make these decisions "in committee" or by one appointed person, both will create difficulties. "Price" seems to create most dissention and it is vital that the marketing proves to all the beneficiaries that the best price was obtained. Two situations come to mind.

I was appointed to market a deceased estate with two sisters and a brother as beneficiaries. I suggested that all "decision-makers" should be present at a meeting to explain the various methods available to them to market the house. It served me right for using such dreadful real estate terminology as "decision-makers" because, according to the beneficiaries, not only were their spouses involved, but also one set of parents-in-law and three neighbors from both sides. "They're involved because they were very good to Mum and we wouldn't do anything they didn't approve of!" So, there I was with a party of 11 – all believing they were, if not "decision-makers", then certainly "involved parties". If I thought talking to them about their choices was difficult, you should have been there when we came to setting the reserve on auction day! Yes, I recommended an auction, as they could not get even close to agreeing on a price to put it on the market. So we took the price off and then had weekly meetings – yes, with all 12 of us – to discuss market feedback.

The three reasons I recommended auction in this case were:

- Group indecision on price
- The attraction "deceased estate" properties have for buyers
- The necessity to show beneficiaries what the market would pay

It's amazing that, once a property is advertised as a "deceased estate", everyone believes that they will get a bargain and it attracts buyers like bees to a honey pot. Of course, the reality is, with so many interested buyers and the attendant competition, often the very top price is achieved by auctioning – by removing the price and allowing competition. I've never understood why people believe that a "deceased estate" means "bargain priced"! Could it be that genuine buyers want to deal with genuine sellers and they know that the beneficiaries will sell?

Setting the reserve was not easy, in spite of our weekly meetings which, as I said, they ALL attended. The people coming through talked between $160,000-$170,000 and they'd had an offer of $163,000, but they had decided to wait until the auction. They just couldn't agree and what amazed me was the influence of the neighbours who were talking about $180,000. I think the beneficiaries deferred to their age and in respect to their late mother. Neighbours are nearly always looking at above-normal market price, as subconsciously they want to protect the value of their own home! Neighbours are often more unrealistic than the owners! So the morning of the auction we had our meeting and I summarised activity, but there was still no agreement on the reserve. Eventually, I suggested they all write their suggestions on a piece of paper and we'd take the average. I was tempted to say we'd pull one figure "out of the hat"! The agreed way was fairer, even if I had never before or since established a reserve this way. The average was $166,480 so they decided on $166,000. Fortunately, it sold for $173,000 so we didn't have to have yet another conference!

The essential part of that transaction was trying to prove to the beneficiaries AND their spouses AND their neighbours what was the right price for the property. I wrote detailed letters to all beneficiaries (and parents-in-law and neighbour!) each week outlining all activity.

By the way, sometimes with a deceased estate property, it can be greatly improved by removing some of the extra clutter that has sometimes gathered if the same person has lived in the home for a long time. Certainly, in the incident just related, all 11 people involved had a garage sale that paid for the advertising. They also tidied up and gave the property a little tender loving care.

I have fond memories of those crazy meetings and like to think all involved were as happy about the transaction as I was. Actually, the neighbours must have been happy as within and months I'd been asked to sell the houses on each side – the ones belonging to the neighbours involved in the sale. Neither auctioned and they were realistic about the price as they had an established benchmark. If you have had a positive experience with an agent, it just makes good sense to use that agent when you want to sell. Certainly I felt as if I were dealing with "old friends" and they were familiar with how I operated.

The above situation – minus the "committee of 11", is probably par for the course when it comes to deceased estates. There will always be a party or parties who are ambitious as to the price and by taking the price off the property altogether it allows totally unprompted market information to be collected.

Recently, I was speaking to a very successful salesperson about the conduct of deceased estate sales and she told a different story. The property is question was in an outer suburb of Melbourne, with again three beneficiaries. This time they decided to just use one of the people involved to make all the decisions.

The designated decision-maker chose the agent and decided that, as the home was an "ex-commission" home in a first-home buyer's market, he would not auction but give the agent a 60-day exclusive agency agreement. The price ($220,000) he wanted to put on the house was probably a little ambitious (euphemism for TOO high) but the agent was happy to try.

Recognising the pull of that "deceased estate" heading, he agreed that it should be advertised in the local paper. The agent held an open home each weekend and in the first three weeks had a lot of inspections, with most attendees commenting on the fact that the price was unrealistic. After three weeks the price was dropped by $5000, which still kept it above what the market was saying. Then came an offer of $205,000, still $10,000 below the asking price. The spokesperson decided against accepting the offer - the agent said that she did ask him to talk to the other beneficiaries but he was adamant that he would make the decision. Eventually, the advertising money was spent and the "deceased estate" drawcard lost its ability to excite buyers. After the 60 days the property was given to another agent. By this time it had been empty for months, was showing signs of neglect and the beneficiaries were tired of mowing and tidying. It was sold six weeks after the second agent started the marketing for $195,000! Evidently, the other two beneficiaries were most unhappy with their nominated spokesperson and family relationships were irreparably damaged.

When marketing any property with multiple ownership, it is absolutely vital that every person involved is confident that the best price has been obtained.

The Chicken or the Egg

So often owners have to try to do battle with the questions, sell first and then start looking, or find a property and then sell. It's what comes first, the chicken or the egg?

The questions all owners will ask themselves are:

- "Do I look until I find something before I sell?"
- "Do I put a contract on a property and hope that my current property will sell in time to finalise?"
- "If I don't, where will I live if the sale finalises before I've found something?"
- "If I find a property that I like and I don't buy it, will it still be there by the time I sell?" Human nature is so perverse that very often if the property is still there by the time you've sold, the thought is: "Why hasn't it sold? Is there something wrong with it?"

- "Do I try to buy something 'subject to sale' of my own property?"

Again no clear-cut answer but here's some advice.

Certainly start looking before you sell to see if the TYPE of property you want is available in an area where you'd like to live. Then, of course, you need to "do your homework" regarding prices that properties sold for. So look, but be VERY careful of committing.

If you are in the financial position – lucky you – of being able to afford to buy and SETTLE (that means pay for) a property without having to sell yours at all, then, of course, it's fine to buy first. If that's the case you can skip the rest of this chapter.

For most of us poor mortals, we need the money from one property to at least help pay for the next. If you're in that category read on and take note! Should your property not sell, the resultant money that you have to borrow could be very expensive money. Can you afford that extra outlay? What could happen is that you may have to accept a lower-than-expected price because you just can't afford to wait for another buyer to surface. Again, it's an expensive exercise.

The biggest concern is "where will I live"? I don't know of any one who has sold their house and ended up without a roof over their head. It's amazing how often sellers do find something they want to buy once they've sold their house. They look harder, at more properties, and with not such inflexible requirements.

Should the worst come to the worst, you can always rent. As a matter of fact this was the case with one of my daughter's friends just a few weeks ago. Between signing the contract and settlement there was frantic activity in an endeavour to buy a property. EVERY weekend was taken at looking at open homes and going to auctions and every weekday was taken up searching the papers. It was very stressful for him – and everyone else! He didn't find anything in the area he'd decided on so he is now renting in another area while he casually looks for something. The interesting thing is that now he's renting in a different area, he's decided that maybe there ARE other areas where he'd like to live apart from that one originally designated suburb. He had been ready to pay TOP price just to get **something** but now he can afford to wait for the right property to turn up at the right price and now in a larger range of suburbs. Of course, he won't want to wait for too long, as he's renting and the market is going up. So the advice I've given him every time I see him is: "Don't wait too long!"

"Subject to sale" is a condition on a contract that is more in favour in some areas than in others. For example, I haven't heard of this being used in NSW or Victoria for years! What it means is that the buyers ask the owners to take their home off the market until they have sold theirs. If the buyer's home doesn't sell within the designated time there is no contract, the deposit is refunded to the buyer and the owner starts all over again. Of course, there are both negatives and positives.

If you're BUYING this way, the contract favours you as, if you don't sell your home, you've lost nothing. Again, as the buyer you must realise that an owner will only accept a contract with this condition if you pay a PREMIUM price. You have to make it worth their while to take it off the market. If you don't mind paying absolute top dollar and you can find an owner who'll accept these conditions, go ahead. I have to say that when you're the seller, I'd rarely recommend you accept a contract with this condition. That's unless your property had been on the market for ages and ages AND they offered top price AND they didn't ask for too long a period in which to get a sale on their property and the buyer's property is easily saleable! It's a contract that favours the buyer over the seller, even with the buyer paying a premium price.

Please be aware of the financial position in which you MAY find yourself if you buy unconditionally before selling. Are you willing to take the risk and endure sleepless nights worrying about what will happen if you don't sell? Are you willing to perhaps accept less to avoid financial loss? I'm not willing to do either so I guess I'd never buy before selling – actually, I don't even trust myself to do a lot of "looking" as I know I'd be tempted. You know that saying, "the easiest person to sell to is another salesperson". Guess what? It's true!

Sell or Rent and Retain

To be or not to be - to sell or keep and rent it out. Again personal circumstances dictate the answer but make sure that you examine all alternatives.

When I say you could retain the property and rent it, I'm surmising you are seriously looking at the possibility. Every agent will tell you of sellers who say: "If I can't get my price, I'll rent it." It's the most common threat of owners. I know because I used it myself. I'd already moved to Melbourne and was auctioning the very large family home. As I said, it was big, on two hectares, complete with pool and dam. It was a most unlikely property to rent, and besides that, I needed the money to buy in Melbourne, but that didn't stop me from saying: "If I can't get $XYZ, I'll rent it, I don't have to sell!" I couldn't believe that I'd actually said that – but I did, and more than once!

So I'm talking here about the real alternatives, not just a threat that you have no intention of carrying through.

I have a friend who did his sums - he's an accountant - and then worked out that if he could get a certain price (top of the market) it would be a better proposition to sell and invest the money. If he didn't get this figure, then he'd be better renting and retaining. He did his homework and checked with a local rental manager as to whether or not it was a rentable property and how much rent he would expect to get. He put the property on the market for four weeks, telling the agent the price he wanted and that he was totally non-negotiable on that figure. It didn't sell so he rented it. It was an unemotional decision based entirely on figures and also on the belief that neither the market nor the rental market would go backwards.

QUESTIONS TO ASK YOURSELF

- Is it a high maintenance property? Of course, if you have either a pool or beautiful garden (or both) you can always add the cost of a pool maintenance person and gardener to the rent, or trust someone to maintain the property as you wish. I know that properties of that quality are rented and I know all my property manager friends will be throwing up their hands in horror at my suggestion that they are not suitable to rent. But it's your choice!

- Is it easily rentable? Again, check carefully with local property managers. They will be honest about its "rentability", as the last thing any property manager wants is to have houses on their books that are difficult to rent. Of course, it's not just whether the property is rentable, it depends, too, on the demand for rentals in your particular area.

- What rent can I get? Again, ask advice from property managers and they'll help as above.

- Will that rent cover the payments on your loan? If it doesn't then can I afford to make up the difference? Don't forget to add rates and insurance and subtract management fees when you're working on those figures. Don't do figures on 100% occupancy – I use 75% just to be sure!

- Will it be likely to increase or decrease in value? You will know if the market in your area is "on the move" or whether prices seem to be falling. So often it's in the latter circumstance that people decide to retain their property. In this case, it needs to be a long-term strategy. If it is likely to increase in value, it may just be a short-term strategy. For example, in hindsight – and we are all very clever in hindsight – I should have retained my Melbourne property and just rented it. It was an easily maintained property, easily rentable and in a desirable area. I bought it the weekend the property market "peaked" and sold it at the bottom of the market. Why didn't I keep it? Because I didn't do my sums and just automatically thought, "I'm moving to Queensland, I need to sell". I watch the prices in that area of Melbourne and keep thinking of the tens (possibly hundreds!) of thousands more it would be worth if I'd kept it.

The last question is the most important one for you and you would need reference to your accountant or financial adviser before making a decision.

- Can I get a greater return and capital gain with my money invested somewhere else?

    Of course, there are times that you may choose not to listen to all that sensible advice from your accountant and just do "what you want to do". I have a holiday unit, which I love, with the best views in the entire world (well almost!). We, my family and I use it some of the time and it's "holiday" rented for the remainder. On paper, I could probably get a better return in another area of investment - but that is not taking into account the joy I get from spending time in something that is MINE. The figures say that for the time I use the unit I could rent one in the same complex and invest the money with a greater return. Renting someone else's unit is not the same feeling - my unit is another home! So you don't always have to be practical, and if you really want to do something, then do it. Money isn't everything!

Remember:

- Is it easily rentable?
- Can I afford the difference between financial commitments and rental?
- Is it a long-term or short-term project?
- Can I get a greater return and capital gain elsewhere?

Extend or Buy

The perennial question is should I extend or should I sell and re-buy? Of course, anyone who gives you a definite answer either way obviously has their own axe to grind. They're either a builder wanting to do the renovations/extensions or the real estate agent wanting to sell your current home and then sell you another one.

Let's take a dispassionate view. Without doubt your most important consideration should first of all be your area. I know throughout this book that you've read "do your own homework". Guess what, I'm saying it again. Do your own homework – by now you know what to do:

- Call on "sold" signs
- Go to auctions and if they don't sell at auction, check later to see what they eventually sold for
- Go to open homes and then check on sold price
- Check on the internet for sold signs

Why do you need to do your own homework – because the first commandment of real estate is DO NOT OVER-CAPITALISE FOR YOUR AREA. There are exceptions, not one that most agents will accept, but I'll go into those later.

Of course, call in a couple of agents but please, please be honest with them. Tell them that you are undecided and not only ask their advice but ask for their opinion of what you could get for your property if you had to sell it TODAY! Tell them that you know that you would expect more if you actually marketed it, but again: "If I did have to sell TODAY, what could I get?" Actually, that's not a figure a lot of people really want to know or a lot of agents really want to tell!

Once you have the figure, subtract the legals and commission and there's your base.

Of course, you have got quotes for extending, haven't you? Don't just guess!

So obtain quotes and add this cost to your base figure. For example, the agent could sell your home for $285,000 today. That's the worst scenario - which is where you should start! Less legals etc, you're left with approximately $270,000 and extensions are going to cost $100,000. Don't guess, get quotes, as all extensions cost more than you think!

A few questions to ask yourself:

1. Have there been any other houses in my area that have sold for $375,000? When?

2. What else is available for $375,000 in an area that I'd like to live in?

3. Are prices in my area increasing or decreasing?

4. Do I care if I over-capitalise?

No.1 - Have any other houses sold in my area for the price of my property, plus the cost of extension? If nothing in your area has ever sold for that price, are you going to over-capitalise for your area? You decided that on black and white evidence. If you decide to ignore that evidence, then that's your prerogative.

No. 2 - What else is available? Go to open homes and get an idea of what property you could buy that would give you the same facilities as your own, plus extensions. Remember to take into account the chaos of extending! At best, by buying a completed project you know what it will look like.

No. 3 - Look at what's happening in your suburb/street. Are houses that are sold being renovated and improved? This is indicative of a change in an area. Just as politicians love to say, "the city is going ahead, look at all the cranes in the sky", so you too can look at the houses being "done-up". Or is the suburb fairly stable with little changes being done to property? If this is the case, you are at greater risk of over-capitalising.

No. 4 - Do I care if I over-capitalise? This is where a lot of real estate agents will disagree with me, but I know from experience that this can be the case. I know because I have over-capitalised on my own home but I did it with my eyes wide open. The position was perfect, within walking distance to two of my married daughters, and with plenty of trees and a well-established garden. I really only want to be very comfortable and I have absolutely NO intention of EVER selling – it won't be sold until it's a "deceased estate" sale! Every time I did some improvement my real estate friends would throw up their hands in horror and say: "Stop spending money here. You're over-capitalising." However, I have been fortunate as I think the suburb may have caught up to me – maybe they caught the renovations "bug" from me! It's become a very in-vogue suburb – which it wasn't as much when I started renovating.

So with your situation, do you want to take a chance that the area will change? Is the position such that it can't be duplicated because of its convenience for you personally?

These are questions that you should consider carefully before making a decision, probably the most important being the problem of over capitalisation. It is an individual situation determined by your own personal circumstances.

What has to be considered:

- Will I get value by selling and buying a larger home?
- Will I over-capitalise if I extend?
- Do I care if I over-capitalise?

Renovate or Titivate? Or Nothing!

As with "deceased estates" the overused heading "renovator's dream" (nightmare more likely) always appeals to the bargain hunters. So when do you perform major surgery and when will cosmetic surgery suffice?

If you've bought a property with the sole purpose of renovating and then re-selling, your course of action is quite clear – start work! So often we see cases of gross over-capitalising with renovations. Cases where properties in an average area are renovated with expensive fittings and there's just no chance of recouping the costs. If you buy a property to renovate, please add all the costs likely to be involved before making a decision to buy or not. That means include legal fees (to buy and to sell), stamp duty, selling commission, interest on capital tied up or payments on the loan, as well as the actual renovating costs. The total of all these outgoings should not make that property more expensive than all the surrounding properties. This sounds so basic yet every real estate agent will have stories to tell about over-enthusiastic "renovators" who have over-capitalised for the area. It is foolish to embark on the above exercise unless you have done extensive homework on prices of properties in the area and how much you'll eventually need to make a profit eg. No matter how small!

Now read the chapter titled "Extend or Buy" as some of the advice given there will also apply to you.

I've been watching a house that I drive past daily and I've always admired. It was sold for $350,000, the kitchen and bathrooms were replaced, a back deck added and it was fenced. It is now on the market for $500,000 – while not over-capitalised for the area it's just too much too ask for the HOUSE! It's now been on the market, in its renovated state, for three months at least, during which time I suspect the investors have had large interest payments. It will eventually sell for considerably below $500,000 and with the interest payments taken into account, unless the investors are careful they'll end up making a loss, all because they were too greedy in the beginning. If it had been put on the market immediately after the changes at $350,000 plus costs involved with renovating and purchasing a moderate profit added, it would no doubt have given them a return. So when renovating, don't be greedy!

By the way, when you do renovate choose fairly neutral colours – something between "boring" and pink and purple! Also, don't forget the garden. People who buy a pristine, renovated home usually don't want a really high maintenance garden so

Renovate or Titivate? Or Nothing!

invest in some paving and lots of pine bark etc. Last, but not least, don't be too greedy.

When do you "titivate" or when do you "renovate" your own home before selling? Or do you do "nothing"?

The basic philosophy and rules applying in the chapter "Extend or Buy" will apply if you are considering the major urgency of renovating your own home – don't over-capitalise.

Let's discuss the "do nothing" situation. My plumber was telling me of a home he'd been working on, which sounded like the chamber of horrors. The outside of this timber home was covered in heavy vines, the verandah rails had rotted and most had "disappeared", the carpet was threadbare and the kitchen and bathrooms were original – i.e. about 50 years old – and the tiles had fallen off the bathroom walls. The whole of the outside area was completely overgrown. I think there were even more problems but that's enough to give you an idea of the property's condition. It needed a massive amount of physical and professional work to even make it livable. The occupant was an elderly (read old!) lady who had lived in it since it was built, and was now moving to a home. The sad thing is that she was spending money on replacing the verandah railings, putting in a new toilet, taking the vines off the home and RE-CARPETTING! At the very least she was spending $10,000 and her chances of recouping that $10,000 would be remote. Who was going to buy this house? Someone who was not afraid of work and wanted to completely renovate it or someone else who was going to demolish and start afresh. So there are times like that when it's best to just do nothing. Let everyone think that because it's a "renovators dream" they'll get a bargain and let them bid against each other!

For the majority of you reading this book and considering selling, it is more likely that the "titivating" will be your best option. I've discussed how best to do this "titivating" in the section "You don't get a second chance."

In summary:

If you totally renovate:

- Don't overcapitalise for area
- Do your homework re: all costs involved
- Don't be greedy

If you are just titivating:

- TLC not dollars
- Cosmetic surgery rather than major surgery!

When do you do "nothing"?

- When the outlay will not be re-couped in the sale

Divorce has Forced the Sale

Unfortunately, many of the sales we see now result from a marriage break-up. If you can possibly bear to be in the same room for even comparatively short periods, it is easier for you both to reach a decision on which agent you want, the marketing and eventually the sale price. Please don't shower the poor real estate agent with animosity. So often both parties disagree with each other just on principle. If relations are such that being in the same room is not practical, then other options need to be considered. The first option is to use the same agent who just goes from one party to the other throughout the programme.

Then, of course, I have known cases where ALL communication – and that meant the decisions from the method of sale to accepting an offer – went through each solicitor. Now that really slows down the works.

Then, of course:

- How will you sell the property in contention?
- Will you advertise?
- Who will pay for the advertising?
- Who decides if an offer is to be accepted?

And most importantly:

- **What is the order of your priorities?** i.e. price, speed of sale and inconvenience.

The "how" factor first. In cases like this it is imperative that the best possible price is obtained as the money obtained is going to be split between two parties. Two people are going to start again with about half of their previous assets. Also, legally there must be no suggestion that anything but the best price was obtained, unless together you've put speed of sale or inconvenience ahead of premium price in your list of priorities.

As for the advertising, the following suggestion is based purely on experiencing this situation with several owners and finding this was an acceptable answer. I'm not saying it is THE answer but if you're in this situation you may like to try it. Sometimes it is the party NOT living in the home who is keenest to sell. The resident party is often happy to stay where they are enjoying rent-free accommodation. I found that it was important first to get the resident half to an agreed way to market. And that was made easier if I'd had prior agreement from the other half to pay for the advertising, and sometimes even the commission, as they were more anxious to dispose of the property. This sounds complicated but it was merely based on the fact that the person who was most anxious to sell was usually the person who wasn't living in the house and so that party was usually more willing to spend money to get the sale going.

In these circumstances I've found auction the most acceptable option to both parties as getting agreement on what price to market the house was absolutely impossible. By the time it came to talk reserve and acceptance of an offer, they both had evidence about the value the market was placing on the property in question.

Should you feel uncomfortable accepting advice from the same person, then why not ask for two people (from the same office) to both be responsible for the sale. This is not the ideal solution as it just involves more communicating and more "toing and froing" (if there's such words!). Be aware of having too many people involved. By the time any message is relayed several times it always becomes distorted. In all cases please don't even try to involve the agent in your personal trauma. If they become too emotionally involved they cannot give you impartial advice.

If the relationship has deteriorated to the extent that even two people from the same office is not acceptable, then use two different agencies - one agent from each for each of you! Complicated but if needs must! Clarify with both agents about the division of the commission before you sign the agreement to sell. You may even prefer to pay full commission to each, but that's up to you.

All this assumes that you are not talking. If you are on friendly terms then approach the sale exactly the same as any other –

talk to and select the agent together and the "how" to market should also be chosen to meet your circumstances.

Just one more thing: if the separation/divorce is in the early stages I can well understand your not wanting to advertise the fact from the rooftop. Practically everyone who goes to an open home or views a house by appointment will ask "why are they selling"? Don't ask me why, but it always appears so vitally important and I was sometimes momentarily tempted to say, "It's none of your business", but, of course, I never, ever would! But it was a temptation! Don't we all have situations where there's an obvious smart answer that we can only DREAM of using? Back to "why are they selling"? The agent should never lie but I found that the best answer was a casual – "just personal reasons". Before the marketing starts, brief your agent on your preferred answer to that question. Too late after the first open home or after buyers have been shown the property. Make sure your agents are prepared with the answer you want.

Your choices in selling:

- Use one agent who will communicate with you separately
- Use two agents from the same office or even two different agencies
- Deal only through solicitors
- Use auction when a price cannot be amicably decided
- Would the non-resident party be willing to be responsible for the advertising?

Netting More Buyers

Let's start with one claim - I have not heard of one reason why the internet must not be used in the listing of your property for sale.

Even if you are the most reclusive and privacy-seeking seller, an internet listing just makes good common sense.

Yes, some properties are selling directly from the internet listing and there are no hard and fast patterns. There are enquiries from expatriates abroad who know the area and often can remember the neighbourhood. Stories such as these are no longer remarkable in a group such as ours.

Enquiries can come from purchasers living virtually a stone's throw away. You can't be sure.

I know of a specific case where the buyer was moving from Auckland to Brisbane. They selected the suburb (just an ordinary suburb) and property wholly from the internet. They then conducted all negotiation via e-mail, the property settled and on arrival they moved straight into their new home! They were determined not to have two moves.

OK, the number of direct sales is limited. But the possibility is always there. The process has become so professional. Good information can be provided with plenty of pictures. Virtual tours giving the sensation of "being there" are increasingly common. Easy contact arrangements for further discussion are all making it increasingly popular for would-be purchasers.

And purchasers do like it. Traffic to our website is exploding, with every month seemingly breaking the record of the previous month! It's apparent that intending and "thinking about it" purchasers are visiting websites in an increasing expectation that they will find important information on property generally - both for property availability and price indications.

Every agent must offer internet exposure. Each agent has a different website strategy. It's worthwhile asking your prospective agent:

- "What is your website offering?"
- "Is there flexibility as to the extent of the exposure to purchasers?"

You can no longer ignore this avenue to source a buyer for your property.

The Flexibility of Auctions

Don't ever let anyone tell you that you MUST advertise in a certain paper and with a certain size.

Don't ever let anyone tell you that you MUST auction "in-rooms" or "on-site".

Don't ever let anyone tell you that you MUST wait until auction day to sell.

Don't EVER let anyone tell you that you cannot auction a property that has already been marketed with a price.

As I have kept reiterating, don't let any agent tell you that you must do anything! Their job is to give you the alternatives and your job is to make the choice.

The purpose of giving you the following examples is to refute those claims that properties marketed by auction must conform to a set position. Auction is a very flexible form of marketing. There's no black and white!

Of course, it is desirable to advertise all property so that it will be seen – I have discussed advertising separately but again every case must be addressed according to its own particular circumstances. Early in my selling career I was called in to a tiny home on a small piece of land by a dear old lady who wanted to sell and move to a caravan park on the Gold Coast. She'd lived in the property all her life and really had no idea of its value. Neither did I! It was a timber home surrounded by brick homes, was on a very small block of land and the house was badly in need of repair. But it had a certain charm. No one in the office could recall any property to use as a benchmark – evidently it was one of the original houses, if not THE original house, in the area. Miss M asked me if I thought that she could get $29,000 for it. Now even in those "olden" days we hadn't seen anything under $45,000 for some time, but then neither had we had seen such a tiny house. While I didn't know what she could get, I was positive it was more than the $29,000 she needed to buy her caravan – that was how she arrived at the $29,000. I discussed the value of auction to establish the price and she agreed with me. We talked advertising and she said she needed to see how much money she had. At this point she went to her wood stove, removed a brick from the side of the fireplace and took out a tin. By the time she'd counted out what was required for rates and electricity I'd made a decision. "Don't worry about advertising, Miss M, I'll work something out." I persuaded our "sign" man to give me a large sign for nothing, put it on her fence and I then adorned the house with flags – it looked like a used car yard but it was on a busy road and sure created lots of interest. Again, it was a most successful auction with more than a HUNDRED people there and it sold for $42,750! When the delighted and emotional Miss M. explained to me that she could now buy an annex for her caravan and for the first time in her life she'd be able to have a telephone – she wasn't the only person in tears! It's times like that when one really loves being in real estate!

There's always that ongoing debate about "in-rooms" or "on site". In-rooms means that the property is auctioned at a selected venue along with other properties. The advantages are that people are always present and the buyers and owners are not as conspicuous. Also, the atmosphere created will encourage the competition between buyers. Professional auctioneers will organise either colour slides or a video of each property, which is shown before that property is auctioned. The auctioneer has the ability to concentrate on the positive aspects of the property – for example, the view or the living area etc. I've found that auctioneers can passionately argue in-rooms v on-site for hours with both sides so often believing there is only one way! As a company, we now do a "mix". There's no right or wrong!

On-site means AT the actual property. Even then, where the auction is actually held varies from area to area. In Melbourne, the home of auctions, most properties are auctioned on-site and on the footpath. Don't ask me why, but traditionally the auctioneer stands on one side of the road with everyone scattered on or across the road in front of the property! I can recall very few Melbourne auctions where the auction was actually held within the perimeters of the property. So all you Melbourne people, if you have a property that you think has an appealing area large enough to hold the attendees, then you don't HAVE to have everyone stand outside. Again the on-site devotees believe that potential bidders may be encouraged to pay more if they're actually at the property. When I have auctioned properties I've used BOTH in-rooms and on-site. Most certainly, my personal investment properties or units I've sold by auction were always in-rooms as there was rarely anything attractive about them!

Look at what is usual for your area. Look at your property dispassionately - has it an atmosphere conducive to encouraging bidders? Talk to your selected agent and then decide. If you have firm views either way, remember you're in charge and it's your choice.

The everlasting dilemma with auctions – should I sell before auction or wait until auction day. This is a time when you must listen to the agent and know the questions to ask:

- "Will the buyers wait until auction day?"
- "Have you any other interested parties?" (Although I must say that any good agent would have contacted every interested person before even bringing the offer to you).

As far as the first question goes, who can tell if someone else will "turn up" by auction day? I have to say that under normal circumstances it's often wise to wait as, without doubt, two or more bidders at an auction will get you the best price. However, as in everything, no two situations are the same.

The Flexibility of Auctions

Let me tell you a story that happened to me personally. I had an investment unit that I'd bought for $100,000 two years before the time in question. I decided to sell and did my research to find that two units in the block of six had sold in the past three months – one for $120,000 and one for $118,000. I was very happy with that information, as I wanted to buy something else as long as I could clear $110,000 ($105,000 at a pinch!). I put it up for auction (of course!), paid for a decent-sized ad in the paper and waited for the agent's call after the first open home. Imagine my delight when she rang me to say that she had two offers, both on signed contracts – one for $120,000 and one for $137,500. The latter wanted immediate settlement – seven days – as a condition of the sale. Why that much? It was a purely emotional decision as she had an ill member of the family who was returning home and wanted somewhere where he could "see the water". I had what someone wanted and, as it was vacant, it was available in the time frame requested. I accepted the terms, of course. Everyone said: "Why didn't you wait for auction day and take advantage of the competition?" The point is that under these particular circumstances that buyer wouldn't have been there by auction day. So every offer must be judged on its own circumstances. This was certainly a case where the "first offer was the best offer", probably $12,000 to $15,000 better than any other offer I was likely to get. The buyer was a real estate agent (from another company) who would have had access to the same information as me about past sales, but when emotion enters the equation, logic goes out the window. I must say, finally, that this is one of my favourite stories because not only does it bear out my belief in the auction system, but it was also my money!

So ask questions of the agent and make your decision. So often when we make a decision we then re-visit that decision again and again. All that anyone can ever do is make a decision based on the facts available at that time. Of course, there will be stories of someone approaching the owner after a deal has been done and saying: "I'd have paid more than that!" I've seen that happen no matter how the property was sold, with a price, without a price, before auction, at auction or after auction. Once you've made a decision, move on. While you're looking back you miss future opportunities.

So many times I've been told "but it's already been on the market with a price and everyone will know what I want". There are countless cases that I could quote to refute this belief but I'll content myself with just one.

A property not far from where I live had been on the market for some time at $330,000. After marketing with a price for some time they really only had three alternatives, didn't they? They could just stay as is, which was hardly a viable alternative, as it hadn't produced any results so far. So what would change now? Or they could reduce the price and hope to attract a different price range buyer. Or they could take the price off altogether and auction. They chose the latter. The agent contacted all the buyers who had already seen it and who hadn't yet bought and said that it was now being marketed without a price. The buyers were invited to have another look and this time without being influenced by price. The buyers now recognised that the owners genuinely wanted to sell. Genuine buyers only want to deal with genuine sellers and genuine sellers only want to deal with genuine buyers. It's the buyers who want to buy NOW who are attracted to auction. They then opened the home for inspection every weekend to attract all the new buyers into the marketplace. To say that "everyone" would know the price was ignoring the fact that new buyers come into the marketplace every week – every day in fact! Then, of course, the buyers who thought that they didn't want to pay more than $300,000 now also came to look. I emphasise the <u>thought</u> as most buyers end up paying more than they first intend to pay. It's human nature with buyers – "let's see if we can get what we want for less and not have to borrow so much". Is that what you did? I have always certainly started looking at less then I eventually paid. The average buyer seems to pay 10-15 % above where they started to look, unless they are very strong-minded! So, by taking the price off altogether, the range of buyers looking at it increased. Real buyers know value so, of course, buyers in the $100,000 to $200,000 range didn't become interested. They ended up on auction day with three bidders, one dropped out at $310,000 and the other two battled it out – or bid it out – to $342,000! The eventual buyer had seen it when it was on the market for $330,000. Just don't even ask me why he hadn't bought it then or was now willing to pay $342,000! The owners didn't question it either; they were happy to just take the money! Wouldn't you be?

It would be very wrong of me to suggest that every property that has been already marketed with a price and then gone to auction will sell above the previously marketed price. Of course, it doesn't often happen but it CAN! As I said earlier, once a property has been unsuccessfully exposed to the market with a price, then the future alternatives are to drop the price, or remove the price altogether. I know of no other way to re-create interest and a subsequent sale.

When/How do You Sell an Investment Property?

I'm not going to write about the best time to capitalise or re-finance etc as this advice is best given by an accountant and every person's financial circumstances are different. My advice is purely from a real estate point of view and my own personal experiences.

There are basically two times to sell – when you'd "sort-of" like to and when you really <u>want</u> to! Let's talk about the first.

Personally, whenever a rental property of mine was vacant I'd instruct the agents to try to sell it but only until another tenant was found. I'd only give a maximum of two weeks. The price I put on the property was at the very top end of the market and really I was only testing the market "just in case"! It cost me only two weeks' rent and a fair few negative reactions from the agents, as it was never their preferred method of marketing – high price and no advertising! Although over the years I have only ever sold one property during a two-week period, I found it a good exercise in finding out what the market was like in an area often a long way from where I lived. Actually, I have been haunted by the thought that I probably undersold that one property, as it sold in a week and at my price. Sometimes we're never satisfied! It is well worth a try if your property is empty and you don't really care if you sell or not. It will only sell if the agent happens to have already identified a buyer that particularly wants that area or type of house/unit.

Then there are the times that you are serious about selling. One hears horror stories about the lack of cooperation from the tenant and how difficult it can be to gain access. I have to say that I have never had this experience. It wasn't because I always had wonderful tenants but because I recognised that it was inconvenient for a tenant to have people coming through when a house was on the market and that they had nothing to gain financially from the transaction. So I gave them a financial interest. I instructed the managing agent to halve the rent while the property was on the market in return for waiving the "24-hour" notice of access. In most areas, tenants need to be given at least 24 hours' notice in writing before any inspection. The managing agent also asked for an acceptable level of tidiness, if applicable. When I've suggested this to landlords, so often the suggestion has been dismissed with "why should I give away half the rent"? At least you're getting HALF, as often the tenants leave as soon as a property goes on the market and there's NO rent coming in. If the property takes four weeks to sell then up to six weeks (or more!) to settle you've lost two to three MONTHS rent! I think it is also fair to promise at least 30 days' notice before the tenants need to move – even if legally they only need one to two weeks if their tenancy agreement has expired. My experience has been that at half rent they stay as long as they can and the property isn't empty, and at least there's some rent coming in.

It's like everything in life; if you try to be too greedy, you end up with nothing!

As for the method of selling in the above circumstances – i.e. where I've wanted to sell, I've always auctioned. I've chosen this method in those circumstances because:

- There is less inconvenience for the tenant with weekly open homes
- It's difficult to accurately ascertain price when you're not in that city/town/suburb
- The longer it was on the market, the more money it was costing me
- The average "days on market" for auction properties are usually less than any other method of marketing

A word about "days on market". This is a greatly ignored area in selling. A good agent will be able to tell you the average time properties stay on the market when auctioned and when listed exclusively. This is important information that will help you make a decision about the method of marketing. As I said, with an investment property, time equals money so I always chose to auction – when I really wanted to sell!

The other area often ignored by both real estate agents and landlords is "vendor finance". Often owners do not need the entire sale price and can afford to finance the sale themselves. Only once did I offer vendor finance and it was to the tenant. They'd been great tenants, who did doing repairs and painting if I paid for the materials, and they didn't want to move. But they didn't meet bank qualifications – although these days, with access to more flexible lending, they'd no doubt be approved for a loan! On advice from my solicitor I held the first mortgage. Their repayments were considerably greater than the rent they'd been paying because, otherwise, there was no point in the arrangement. After several years they had enough equity to re-finance with a building society. Sometimes it is just a matter of leaving a few thousand dollars in as vendor finance. I must stress here that under these circumstances you must be advised by your accountant and protected by an agreement drawn up by your solicitor. This is NOT a time to do your own legals. Please seek advice before making such an offer – it just happened to suit me and it worked out perfectly.

While we are speaking about rental properties, I must strongly advise against managing the property yourself. Anybody can find a tenant but it's the ongoing management that requires the professional expertise of trained property managers. I believe that the letting fee is probably the very best money you can spend in regards to investment properties. Do you really want to be woken at 1.00am because their hot water system has burst or the toilet is blocked or the rain has ruined the carpet? Do you really want to front the rental tribunal with all of the attendant letters to try to recover lost rent? Do you really want to have to prove to the rental bond authority that you needed to keep half of the bond because the property was left dirty? Do you want or have time to do any or all of the above? Property managers earn every cent of their fees. You should ask for a written inspection report every six months at least and to be advised as soon as a tenant is in arrears.

Don't necessarily "shop around" for the agency with the lowest management fees. Shop around for the agency that offers you the best service and again will guarantee that service. To make a decision to use a property management agent purely on the basis of the management fee involved is very foolish. Don't gamble valuable income to save a few dollars.

In summary:

- Test the market whenever the property is empty
- Offer the tenants consideration to gain their cooperation
- Auctions are less hassle for tenants
- Don't even THINK of managing your own rental properties!

What Could Happen

In the next few chapters I have taken six examples of owners with different needs and living in different types of areas. I have followed their journey right from deciding to sell to finalising the sale.

This has been done to allow you to identify with the situations in which they find themselves and perhaps learn from their solutions. Not for one minute do I think that anyone will identify with all six situations, just as I can't imagine anyone identifying totally with all of one group's experiences. Take something from each! The people are fictitious but I've collated their journey from my real estate experiences.

These anecdotes will show again that to say that there is only one way to market a property is wrong and it is important to recognise that different circumstances and properties require different strategies.

While following these groups of people it will become obvious that there is a process involved when selling residential property – a series of events that should happen.

The process is as listed below:

1. The initial meeting is when you call in the agent to look at the house and you have a chance to look at the agent. All of the owners do not have to be present at this time.

2. The next meeting is the marketing presentation when the agent explains to you all the options available to you to market your home, and you will sign an agency agreement. However, if all owners are present at no. 1, these first two areas MAY be combined.

3. If you have several agents giving you a marketing presentation, you will probably listen to all and then advise the selected agent of your choice.

4. Then you can expect inspections by buyers. Inspections will occur through an "open home" program or by appointment with the agent.

5. Once you get an offer, the negotiating process starts. Not every offer results in a sale.

6. Between the signing of the contract and the settlement there is normally a time of between 30 and 90 days.

7. Settlement is effected between the solicitors/conveyancers acting for the owner and those acting for the buyer.

Case Study 1 - Hugh and Samantha Thomas

Hugh and Samantha have made the decision ... they will have to forgo their café latte society in favour of a more suburban lifestyle. After all, with the birth of their first child in six months, the three levels and small paved courtyard that they loved would hardly fit a pram let alone a toddler. So ... what next?

This was their first home and so they had no idea how to even start the daunting process of selling. They have noted that houses in their area sell fairly quickly - in fact, no sooner does the sign go up than there seems to be a big "SOLD" slash across it.

- Their parents said: "Get in three or four agents."

- Their friends said: "We know someone."
- Their work mates said: "I'd auction it."
- Their postman said: "Don't auction it."
- Their cousins, their greengrocer, their newsagent

.... And, in fact, **everyone** had a different opinion.

As a dutiful daughter Samantha listened to her mother who advised her to get in three agents and have the house looking at its best when each agent arrived. She put flowers in the living area, turned on the light in the darkish second bedroom and put a chequered tablecloth and fruit on the table in their courtyard. It all looked very inviting. What a pity to sell it, she thought!

All three agents arrived on time and each was enthusiastic about the house and felt that it was a very saleable property. She asked each one about the expected price and two felt they'd like to go back to the office to look up some comparable sales in the area and come back with a full recommendation as to marketing and possible expected price. One agent did give a range between $450,000 and $500,000, which Samantha felt was not enough and was too big a difference in range. The agent casually remarked that, of course, she'd "have to auction, that's all we do", and then, to add insult to injury, added, "but I'll talk to your husband about that" – how to lose friends and antagonise possible clients in one easy lesson. He really was most unprofessional and so Samantha said she'd call him as they weren't quite ready to sell. What a surprise he'd get in a week or so when he drove past and saw the "For Sale" sign, if of course he ever drove past. Samantha did the right thing to dismiss him.

Case Study 1 - Hugh and Samantha Thomas

I've found "I'll call you later" is just great to get rid of a pushy or uninterested salesperson. This is just another version of the "don't call me, I'll call you" brush-off. Just remember, you have every right to deal only with people with whom you are comfortable.

BOTH the other agents rang Samantha to confirm their appointment (the sign of a professional approach) and one, recognising her inexperience in selling, had even suggested that if she were seeing more than one agent she should allow at least an hour between appointments.

When it came to the actual method of marketing both of the other agents, David and Mark, explained the difference between marketing with a price and without a price. But they also recommended auction for their area, as it was the accepted and almost expected method of marketing for that area of the city. One recommended "in-rooms" as the preferred venue for the auction and the other recommended the auction be "on site" because it was such a charming exterior. However, both being professional agents, stressed that it would be Hugh and Samantha's choice as to where the auction was held.

David, the first agent, presented a professionally prepared "marketing submission" showing a recommended advertising schedule, with samples of past advertising and testimonials.

Mark's submission contained the above information, plus his testimonials included a list of some phone numbers from past owners who had given him permission to make the offer to phone them. He also showed them the company's considerable website on his laptop. Both Samantha and Hugh were very comfortable with the net and realised its great potential. David, from a smaller agency, did not have as active a website and in his presentation, he did not include details of the number of viewings to the site.

There was still some confusion in Hugh's and Samantha's mind as to price.

As they'd decided to auction there wasn't any immediate urgency in deciding on price. Mark had suggested a range of $530,000 to $560,000 (which Hugh took to mean that Mark probably thought about $545,000 - in the middle!) while David suggested $530,000 to $540,000. Both showed recent sales in the area to justify those figures. Mark gave them the addresses of those sales so they could drive past and at least get an idea from the exterior how it compared with their terrace house. While their property was on the market they decided that they would do some investigative work of their own. They would

- Go to open homes and when sold they'd follow up and ask for the selling price
- Phone every agency that had a "sold" sign and again ask for details and selling price
- Look at the various internet sites and phone the agents about prices properties sold for

(Obviously they had read my book and the many references to deciding on a price.)

Of course, both agents had pointed out that it was an auction so the buyers in the market would establish current market value, no matter what the agent said. Our nervous owners still wanted a vague idea as they wanted to start looking for something with more room and needed to know approximately the price range they should consider. Both David and Mark had given sufficient information and they hoped their own research would back those figures.

They listened to both the agents, separately of course, then perused the marketing submissions that both left. It was hard to decide but in the end it was Mark's understanding that Samantha wanted as little disruption as possible and his unbounded enthusiasm for the house, the area and his job that gave him the final edge. Look for an agent who will LISTEN and is ENTHUSIASTIC! If they'll listen to you then they'll listen to buyers and be able to more easily recognise the buyer for your home. They rang Mark with their decision the next morning and he made an appointment for the next evening to complete the necessary paper-work that would enable him to start marketing the property. As a courtesy David was also contacted. Samantha was glad David was out and so she could just leave a message. Hugh and Samantha are in an area where properties for sale are advertised extensively and the two media used are their metropolitan paper and a very popular, well-produced, local real estate-dominated publication. As their metropolitan paper wasn't in colour they used a sketch for that ad and several large colour photographs in the other publication. The exterior of their terrace, while attractive, was similar to lots of other exteriors, so they used that as a smaller photo in the ad, with the main photo of their back terrace, which was partly covered. They made an instant garden with pots of flowering plants and had the area looking comfortable and inviting.

Their agent advised that their dominant advertising should be in the coloured magazine/paper with less use of the metropolitan paper. The specific company coloured magazine certainly warranted being included as this was circulated to qualified buyers and database contacts of the agency.

A "photo" signboard was used featuring, again, the attractive back terrace.

The full page in the company magazine was used as a brochure to be dropped at open homes and to be sent to possible interested people – for example, attendees of other open homes. Over the next couple of days, Mark submitted ads for approval and set the times for the open homes. Wednesdays and Saturdays were the times appropriate for that area.

Nothing, but nothing prepares owners for the nervous anticipation of the very first open home. Hugh and Samantha's butterflies were eased with delivery of a floral arrangement on the Saturday morning of their first open! It was from Mark, wishing them a successful open home. It gave them confidence in their choice of an agent. But the nervousness was still there, "Will anyone come?" "Will someone absolutely fall in love with it and make a fantastic offer?" Thoughts like that are normal – so many people are optimists, why else would so many of us buy lotto tickets!

All the open homes were a great success with up to 30 people at the weekends and often 10-15 at on Wednesdays. Each week, Samantha had the house looking most inviting with flowers (from Mark), soft music and lightly fragranced oil burners.

Case Study 1 - Hugh and Samantha Thomas

The information from the agent was that most people were talking $540,000, with no one above $550,000. As they were in an area (NSW) where buyers took contracts to peruse, they had a rough idea of the number of interested parties. There were eight contracts "out" before auction day. In other words eight couples had asked for copies of the contracts, expressed interest, and in some cases had pest and building reports done. One couple had offered $535,000 but the agent had recommended, and Hugh and Samantha agreed, that they'd wait to see what happened at the auction.

Hugh and Samantha had a written report from the agent each week and regular meetings to discuss those reports. The agent, Mark, had done all he had promised but come auction evening they were still nervous. The auction was held "in rooms", not at the actual house. They'd had discussions with Mark as to whether it should be "on site" (at the house) or "in rooms" (at a very nice local hotel and at the same time as other auctions) and decided "in rooms".

The market was confident and so were Samantha and Hugh. They set the reserve at $550,000. There's no need to describe exactly how an auction is conducted as I'm sure, like me, you have watched those exciting TV shows. The bidding slowed down at $565,000 with only two bidders left and Hugh and Samantha were barely able to contain their excitement. Very carefully the auctioneer coaxed bids from both bidders with the final and winning bid being $570,500 – SOLD! Not only could Samantha and Hugh buy what they wanted but they also had enough over for another car for Samantha.

To say that auction in every area is as spectacularly successful as this one would be deceitful. The above situation was the perfect criteria for the perfect auction and it DOES happen, probably more often than you hear!

IN SUMMARY:

Hugh and Samantha lived in an area where:

- Auctions were accepted and expected
- The buyers expected properties to be advertised and so not to advertise was suicidal
- Buyers used open homes as their preferred method of inspection

Just remember if they'd only listened to the agents, even with their market research, they would have sold in the MID $500K's – $20,000 below the eventual selling price.

These were typical of sellers whose priorities are:

1	**Best possible price**
2	Shortest time
3	Privacy/least inconvenience and no publicity

Case Study 2 - Mary Gray

Mary is a young, professional involved in marketing who has decided to sell her tiny unit in order to buy something bigger and with room for a small dog. Her current unit is her first home.

Before putting her unit on the market, she went looking at what was available, using open homes to get an idea of what was on the market in her area. She didn't want to move more than one suburb away. At the open homes, Mary spoke to the agents and asked questions about likely sale price etc. She was particularly impressed with one salesperson, Anne, who, after meeting her at an open home, had rung her several times with suggestions about properties she should see. Some of the agents asked if she was interested in the property she visited and when she replied in the negative, they lost interest in her.

After several weeks of open homes, Anne suggested that she could perhaps come to Mary's unit and give her a rough idea of how much she might get for it. Mary had already worked out that she'd need to get close to $300,000 and felt also, from what she'd seen, that this was not beyond the realms of possibility. Anne made an appointment and agreed with Mary's thoughts on price. They talked about selling, but Mary was determined to see if there was anywhere available where she could live before she put her unit on the market. She had enough money to put down a deposit and had organised to borrow an extra $100,000 on top of her mortgage. She decided just to "look" a little more before putting her unit on the market. She wouldn't "buy" until she'd sold her unit.

Then she fell in love – with a townhouse! It was just a few streets away, on the high side of the street, and had an extra bedroom and room for a small dog. She hadn't intended buying right then but it was so perfect and there was also a lot of interest in the property, which was on the market at $400,000. The agent explained that he already had one offer to present to the owner after the open home finished. He also explained that Mary was also entitled to make an offer and he would take both offers to the owner and allow them to decide which contract he would accept. Of course, Mary's dilemma was: "Should I put in an offer." "Yes", she decided, as she felt this townhouse was perfect.

"Would the seller accept an offer subject to the sale of her property?" The agent explained that this would be most unlikely as the owner was anxious to move interstate and in fact the agent felt that it was unlikely that he (the owner) would consider a settlement over 30-40 days.

"How much should I offer? I want it so much," Mary said.

"Can I really get $300,000 for my property?"

"If I can't get $300,000, can I afford to borrow more?"

The agent also explained that the fairest situation was that neither buyer knew what the other offered and both should put in their best offer, as they might not get the chance to increase it.

Mary couldn't help but feel that if the buying was so traumatic, how would she manage the emotion of selling? Normally a confident person, Mary still felt a little "out of her depth" and then remembered Anne, the agent who had been so attentive. A quick call on her mobile, the position explained and Anne suggested that she offer $402,000, with settlement in 40 days. She suggested $2000 above the listed price, in case the other contract had similar conditions but only offered the "asking" price of $400,000. And if that was the case, then the extra $2000 could be important. Anne also allayed Mary's fears about the saleability of her property but did emphasise that she could not guarantee $300,000 and Mary must consider the possibility that she may have to borrow more. "Was that possible?" Anne asked, and Mary certainly hoped so!

The agent presented both contracts to the owner of the townhouse, who decided that the extra $2000 was worth the 10 days extra (30 days compared to 40 days) that Mary had asked for before the property settled. Mary, who was delighted, phoned Anne and they met the next day to plan an aggressive marketing strategy.

Mary's almost twin priorities were speed of sale and price. She had no qualms whatsoever about privacy and was willing to put up with as much inconvenience as necessary. She decided to market her unit without a price for 10 days and then, if it weren't sold, she'd reconsider her selling strategy.

As Mary was involved with marketing, she fully recognised the need to advertise and requested prominent ads in the metropolitan paper. The company Anne worked for had its own weekly magazine and Mary was happy to take a full page in that too. It was full steam ahead as a sale was vital. Mary also had a large signboard with a photograph showing the beautifully appointed interior.

Then came open homes. With her priorities it was essential that Mary get as many people through as quickly as possible to try to identify a buyer who would pay a price acceptable to her. It was decided to open her unit each Saturday and Wednesday afternoon (usual for that area) and Thursday evening (6.00pm to 7.00pm), which was unusual for the area. The view was great – especially at night – and Anne felt that they just might catch some people on their way home from work, hence opening for one hour instead of the usual half-hour.

The first two open homes on the Saturday and Wednesday attracted 21 attendees, but there were no offers and Mary was panic stricken! Then agent Anne arrived on Thursday evening to find that Mary had set out glasses, wine, soft-drink and savouries for her "guests". She was most impressed, as were the eight couples who attended and lingered to enjoy the view and cool breezes. One couple, who had seen the ad in the company magazine delivered to them that morning, made an offer of $280,000 with 30 days settlement and no conditions – 30 days coincided exactly with Mary's settlement on the townhouse that she'd bought.

It was imperative Mary speak again to her finance broker who re-negotiated her borrowing to cover the extra she'd have to pay, plus stamp duties and the price difference (minus agent's fees) from what she had expected for her home and the current offer. Don't forget to include all extras when you're re-financing – for example, legal fees and stamp duties when buying and legal fees and agents' fees when you're selling.

In the meantime, Anne had checked with the other attendees to see if any of them wished to make an offer. One person murmured something about $270,000 but with multiple conditions.

Anne did advise Mary that further open homes could easily, and even probably, produce more buyers. However, by now Mary was terrified that she may not be able to sell at all and so be unable to settle on the next property. Speed of sale was so important that she did not even dare change the offered price by even one dollar in case the buyers changed their mind!

She had advertised extensively so that as many buyers as possible saw her property. This time the buyer came from a company magazine rather than the newspaper – she was not in a position to try to "guess" where the buyer would come from so she covered all bases.

In Mary's case she had to weigh the slightly higher re-payments against the security of having a sale and that sale settling at the most convenient time for her.

Perhaps she could have got more – who knows?

That same reason for acceptance of an offer keeps surfacing – if you can afford to take the offer and it allows you to get on and do what you want to do with your life, it's worth it!

Speed became the dominant priority for Mary:

1	**Shortest time**
2	Best possible price
3	Privacy/least inconvenience and no publicity

Case Study 3 - Bill and Joan Jones

Bill and Joan have four children and a fairly hefty mortgage on their current home. Bill's parents have become frail, so it was decided that it would be best if they combined resources and built a larger home with a special self-contained area for the parents. They have been able to buy the land and do quite a bit of the building before selling.

They've noticed that a lot of homes in the area have "For Sale" signs and some stay on the market for months before sold.

When they moved from the country 15 years ago, they had sold their house there by giving it to three agents. It hadn't been a happy experience. They'd dropped the price quite a lot and then, after they'd signed the contract, one of the other agents said that he'd had a buyer who would have paid more. He was with another agency and Bill and Joan didn't know about the other person's interest. It was disappointing and also confusing as there seemed to be salespeople from all the agencies at first and then no one! And no one took the responsibility of communicating market information to them – Bill and Joan always seemed to be phoning agents asking what was happening.

This time, they were determined to avoid those mistakes but they wondered which agent they should choose, as they knew no agent personally.

How could they tell who was successful?

What price should they ask? They certainly didn't want to "undersell" their house.

So, as Hugh and Samantha did, they called in three agents and made appointments over two evenings.

Agent No. 1 explained that the market was "tough" and there weren't many buyers around – it's a "buyers' market" he said. All of this hardly instilled confidence into Bill and Joan. He also imparted the information that most people wanted a large living area while theirs was quite small – Joan had always thought of it as "cosy"! He wasn't really considered as they found him far too depressing. "You'll never get over $190,000" were his parting words!

Agent No. 2 arrived 15 minutes late – if an agent is not going to be organised enough to get to **this** appointment with you on time, the chances are they are going to be disorganised in lots of other ways. She was very pleasant but spent a lot of time denigrating other agencies and their methods – "open homes don't work", "don't pay for advertising" and "auctions are cons"! In fact, most of her presentation consisted of saying what they **shouldn't** do, with few positive recommendations except that they should give her the listing. She was quite complimentary about the house and recognised the "cosiness" of the living area. She felt that compared with other sales in the area, they should be able to get "in excess of $200,000". As Joan and Bill counted a bottom line $190,000 to $200,000, this sounded good news. But always be wary of anyone who has to denigrate other agents in order to stress their point of view.

Agent No. 3 – Colin brought with him a folder containing his own personal profile, as well as facts about his office, the company of which his office was part, a list of recent sales and a copy of some of his advertising. By the time they had read this, Bill and Joan felt that they knew more about him and they were certainly impressed with his professionalism.

Colin explained how real estate had changed from when they'd sold their last home, 15 years ago. There are now fewer "open" listings. So they realised that, by giving it to one agency, they wouldn't have the same problem as last time – another agency with a buyer who'd pay more. Colin assured them that it was his responsibility to know what every potential buyer for their property was thinking. He explained that **he** would be responsible for regular communications with them. Then, to cement his commitment, he offered a Service Guarantee – a guarantee to do as he'd promised and if he didn't, they could cancel the agency agreement. Realising that professionalism really counts, they decided to give Colin exclusive rights to sell their property for 60 days. They decided to "test the market" at

$220,000 with the proviso that they'd meet Colin in a week's time to review the situation.

As far as price went, he was happy to market the house at whatever price they said as long as they realised that, once the marketing started, they must "listen to the market". It was very comforting for them to hear him say: "It is your right to determine the price it initially goes on the market. I'll endeavor to get your price, but once we have buyers through, we will both have to listen to them."

Bill and Joan's house was in a less expensive bracket, and as they weren't auctioning the property, they needed to budget for a possibly longer time on the market. The response from their free local paper was better than in some areas but, of course, still only had local circulation. The larger papers attracted buyers from a more diverse area within that city, as well as out-of-town buyers. So Joan and Bill, with a smaller budget, decided on a smaller ad in the metropolitan paper for the first and third weeks and one in the local paper on the first, second and fourth weeks. The arrangement was to review the response after that and plan their strategy based on that response. They realised that they would need to do more advertising if it didn't sell but were happy to review the situation after the first few weeks.

Then there was the signboard. There were no "picture" boards in the area (which I always think is a good reason to have one!) and they were on a very tight budget. Colin discussed the merits of having a photo board but when they all looked at what would make a good photograph – there was no pool, no private garden and no exceptional living area. So it was decided to have a large sign with some of the features of the property listed.

- Five bedrooms
- Two living areas
- Huge kitchen

They felt that it was a home for a large family so they emphasised the features that would appeal to a large family. This was also to be the thrust of the media advertising – "Room to move" and "If your family is too big for your current house" etc. They'd emphasise the amount of room inside and outside with 1000sm of land.

Bill and Joan were disappointed with the reaction of buyers at their first open home. Their agent, Colin, relayed the news that most who came through were buyers in the $200,000-plus range – as it was advertised at $220,000 – and were disappointed, feeling that it should have been under $200,000 and closer to $190,000. So, armed with this information, they reduced the price to $210,000 and promised Colin they'd review in another two weeks. After three weeks and now with only one weeks advertising left, Bill and Joan took Colin's and the market's advice and put the price at $198,000. The reaction of this open was more positive but no buyers - every open home doesn't produce a buyer, unfortunately.

By now the advertising budget was exhausted so Bill and Joan decided to try a couple of weeks with no advertising and see what happened. Colin conducted one open home during this period by personally contacting everyone who had been through each of the previous open homes. Three people attended but no joy!

They then decided to look at the advertising week by week and agreed on a smaller ad in both the metropolitan and local paper, again emphasising the size of the home. Their first offer was at $190,000, subject to finance, pest control and building inspection – the buyers borrowing $160,000. This seemed a lot to Bill and Joan who had never borrowed that much in their life!

It's amazing how a property can sit on the market for ages and as soon as one person wants it, so does someone else. Someone from the other side of the city saw the metropolitan ad "Room to grow" and decided that this property may just suit them as they had sold their three-bedroom home because it was too small. They hadn't intended moving to the other side of town but hadn't been able to find what they wanted for what they could afford. Colin advised Bill and Joan not to make a decision on the first contract as these people had an appointment for the next day. The second lot of buyers arrived, inspected the house and felt that it was better value than anything else that they'd seen. The buyers understood that they would need to make a quick decision and they did! Originally, they hadn't wanted to spend more than $180,000 but they made an offer of $190,000 subject to finance and borrowing only $50,000. They perused the pest and building reports that Bill and Joan had already obtained and decided that those reports would suffice. This made the second contract more acceptable but Colin, to be fair, approached both and asked for their BEST offer. The first came up to $196,000, (borrowing $165,000) which made Bill and Joan even more nervous, still with the pest and building conditions and 60 days' settlement. The second came to $194,000 with settlement in 30 days and still only subject to borrowing $50,000. Bill and Joan preferred this contract and felt the shorter settlement and better conditions made up the difference. So they accepted. Finance was approved in just a few days and they prepared to move in with Bill's parents while they finished building. Both assured Colin that when it came time to sell his parent's home, Colin would be contacted. Again, if an agent has given good service, why change?

What happened:

- The best selling time was not productive, as the price was too high.
- The early advertising attracted buyers more than $200,000 while it sold to the $180,000 - $190,000 price range buyers.
- At least Bill and Joan had proved that they couldn't get their original $220,000 although, in their hearts, they had always thought $195,000 - $200,000.

Their priority was certainly obtaining the best price, even looking for a premium. Neither speed of sale nor publicity was a concern. In fact, they were willing to sacrifice some time to make sure that they got the best price.

1	**Best possible price**
2	Shortest time
3	Privacy/least inconvenience and no publicity

Case Study 4 - Tom and Joanne Black

Tom and Joanne are moving. Tom has been transferred interstate so it is imperative that they get a fairly quick sale. Homes in this area seem to stay on sale for a month or two or three before selling. Some are auctioned, some aren't.

The agent (Sue) who sold them this house also sold their last home. She personally delivered some flowers on the day they had moved in and she has always sent Christmas cards and a note on the anniversary of their sale. They really would like to deal with her again as they feel she understands their needs – and they are very comfortable with her. So, with a quick call, they explained their situation and Sue made an appointment to talk to them both that night.

They did not have time to do their own research into sales in the area so they were going to be totally reliant on Sue's suggestion as to price. The choice of the agent was not a problem as they had been delighted with Sue's service before – "when you're on a good thing, stick to it".

Their main concerns were, at what price should they put it on the market and how and where would it be advertised? Sue spent considerable time explaining the positives and negatives of each of the marketing options, with or without a price. She stressed that it was their choice. You must realise that the way you market your home is your choice. It's not like Henry Ford with his "You can have any colour, as long as it's black". It's your home and your choice.

Sue felt between $260,000 and $280,000. Without any real basis for their belief, Tom and Joanne felt they'd like to get closer to $290,000 and so decided to put it on the market at $315,000. Sometimes, owners add extra to the agent's suggested price, just on principle! Tom wanted to "test the market" and Sue preferred to auction as time was limited, the house was well presented and was in an area where people were buying and renovating. So they compromised. They would advertise it for one weekend at $315,000, and if it hadn't sold they'd move into an auction programme. The advertising for that weekend concentrated on the main metropolitan paper hoping that an "out-of-area" buyer might surface and pay Tom's premium price. They used a sign with a photograph of the private pool that couldn't be seen from the front of the house. Sue had two inspections, both by appointment, before the weekend. Neither prospects that Sue brought to the house was interested enough to make an offer, although neither rejected it out of hand. Both thought that it didn't compare in value with other properties that they'd seen. The weekend open home resulted in five couples attending. Sue said this was about average for the area. Sue contacted each attendee after the open home and she then had her meeting with Tom and Joanne.

Seven groups in all had attended. They all compared it to other properties they'd seen and it was found lacking in comparable value – in other words, they all thought the price was too high. It's so strange, once buyers think a property is priced too high they can't look further than that price. I don't think they even see the other positive features.

So now it was time to plan the auction. Together, they worked out an advertising programme. The metropolitan paper had a colour real estate section that had become the most accepted place for buyers to look. This, therefore, became their main focus. They decided on a larger ad for the first week and then, because of budgetary restrictions, they settled for a slightly smaller ad on the third and fourth weeks. Agent Sue also recommended having two pictorial ads in their local free paper. These were far less expensive than in the metropolitan paper but also had a more restricted area of circulation.

Sue also called the small group who had already seen the property and explained the change in strategy. She asked each to re-visit at the first open home and look at the property with the new aspect of no price to cloud their thoughts.

First open home in the auction programme – nine groups – a great result according to Sue. Two of the groups were people who had seen the property previously. Two groups stayed for quite a while (good sign!). Sue said their thoughts on price varied from $260,000 to $280,000, with no one even close to the magic $300,000 let alone the original $315,000, which Tom now recognised as over optimistic.

The next couple of weeks were much the same. The attendees varied from two to six. Sue decided to open the house once in the middle of the week – not usual in that area – and invited all the previous attendees to come "for a second look". It was a hot day so she asked Joanne to have some iced water, cordial and glasses in the kitchen. Sue only had three groups through – two had seen it before and one was a "new" person – and so she had time to give them cool drinks, which meant that they lingered a little longer. It's not possible to give this sort of attention at normal home opens as there are too many people around but, as this was more of a "one-off", it worked very well.

After this open they had an offer of $265,000. Tom and Joanne had to look at it carefully and even consider the possibility that the buyer wouldn't wait until auction (he'd indicated that he wouldn't but…) and even then they may not get more than that at auction. They decided to wait. Never for one minute did Joanne and Tom question Sue's commitment to the property and they felt it was the three of them against the world! The couple who had made the offer had said that they would attend the auction but definitely would never bid - "don't like auctions and our top price is $265,000".

By auction day the Blacks had 27 groups of people who had seen their home. Sue pointed out that to have, in just four weeks of intense activity, more than 27 groups seeing the prop-

Case Study 4 - Tom and Joanne Black

erty in an area where properties didn't sell really quickly, was an excellent result.

Now it was auction "eve" and time to talk about the reserve. Eventually it was decided on a reserve of $290,000 – still a little ambitious! Setting a reserve too high is just the same as putting a property on the market at too high a price. With the latter you waste the valuable first couple of weeks' interest and with the former you waste the interest and competition of the actual auction. Auctions are fascinating and attract people like magnets. In Melbourne whenever there was an auction in our street, the whole street turned out. You could tell which were the locals – they were all sipping a glass of red wine! I think the fascination of the actual auction lies in it being the culmination of weeks of hard work and the intense emotion born of the necessity of both buyers and sellers to make a decision. Few people outside real estate get the chance to witness the fun of negotiation, except at auction, and a lot of the time that's all an auction is – "negotiating in public". With such a powerful combination of emotions, it's no wonder people are attracted to the spectacle.

However, back to the Blacks. Quite a few of the people who had attended the open home turned up, including the couple who had made the offer and two who had seen it three times. Of course, there were a few neighbours who are always anxious to keep abreast of property prices in their area. After all, what that property sells for directly reflects and affects the price of their own property.

The auctioneer opened the bidding with his own bid of $200,000. This was clearly stated as an "auctioneer's bid on behalf of the owners" and all that was saying was, "if no one will pay more than $200,000, we, the owners, will buy it back for that price". Again it's just letting the public know that they wouldn't accept $200,000. It's the same as if a buyer had presented a contract for $200,000 and had said, "if that's all you'll pay, we'll keep it, you'll need to offer more".

Bidding increased, first in $10,000 increases, then in $5000, and finally in $1000 bids to $280,000, where it stalled. The couple who had offered $265,000 (and would NEVER bid) bid to $279,000. Were they not serious when they said that $265,000 was their top price, or did they just get carried away?

Despite Sue talking to each of the groups who had bid (negotiating in public!) no one was willing to offer more. The top bidder explained that he had finance approved only to $280,000. It was time to speak to Tom and Joanne – time for the locals to quickly grab another glass of wine, for the interested parties to experience an increase in their level of anxiety and for the TV stations to take a commercial break! Both Tom and Joanne were definite that it wasn't enough so the property was passed in and offered to the highest bidder at the reserve price of $290,000. This bidder signed a contract offering $285,000, subject to his obtaining the extra finance. Tom and Joanne countersigned the changes and initialled the contract at $290,000. The bidder then offered $288,000, Tom and Joanne agreed and the deal was done, subject to three days finance. After three days Sue advised the owners that the extra finance had been approved and so they could now prepare to move.

So, to summarise, the course of the sale.

- They now had a sale at $288,000 and were very confident that was the best in the market at that time.
- More than 20 different groups of people had inspected their property, which was more than could have been expected by any other method.
- The sale had taken 31 days from start to finish (including the seven days it had marketed with a price). The average days on market for exclusive listings in that type of area would have been about 45-60.

While this is merely an example, I am sure that many people will relate to the circumstances and subsequent events – they're about what one would expect.

The lesson to be learnt:

- If you want to "test" the market, don't waste too much time
- An effective advertising schedule will produce results

Again, speed of the sale and price were important, with perhaps more emphasis on the time.

1	**Shortest time**
2	Best possible price
3	Privacy/least inconvenience and no publicity

Case Study 5 - Agnes and Jack Smith

Agnes and Jack had lived in their current home for 30 years and had now decided to move to a retirement home. They were uneasy at the prospect of having to go through the process of choosing an agent so asked their son Joe to assist them.

Joe asked three agents to come and look at the property and then phone him with their ideas about price. The main requirements for his parents were that they were inconvenienced as little as possible and they would get a price that enabled them to get a nice unit in the village they'd selected. They were quite happy to wait for a good price.

When Joe spoke to each agent he got quite different information.

Agent no. 1 -   "Put on the market between $240,000 and $260,000 and wait for offers"

Agent no. 2 - $240,000 to maybe $250,000

Agent no. 3 - $200,000 to $220,000

So not a lot of help – from $200,000 to $260,000. As I've kept saying, price is such an individual perception.

From the homework Joe had done with sales in the area he'd had in his mind somewhere in the middle of that range. He arranged for each of the agents to return to talk to his parents and himself over the next couple of evenings.

Agent No. 1 was starting at a distinct disadvantage as, at that first inspection, he had tried to tell Agnes and Jack that they should sign an "agreement to sell" right then and there rather than wait to talk to their son. "It's your house!" the agent said. Joe was tempted not to even make another appointment, but his parents reminded Joe that this agent had given the "highest quote"!

No need to go into the details of what these meetings may have entailed, except to say that the agent (no. 2) was selected because she listened to all three of them. She was interested in where they were going and understood that it was more important to wait for the best price than to move quickly. She understood that neither Agnes nor Jack liked the idea of "strangers going through their house". She explained the options available to them, with a price or without a price, and that as they'd expressed distaste for open homes, there was no need to have their home open.

Case Study 5 - Agnes and Jack Smith

Together, they decided on a programme to suit Jack and Agnes.

- Try $250,000 for a while and see what happens.
- A "For Sale" sign – "but not too big"!
- No open homes.
- An advertisement (with photo) in the local paper every two weeks for six weeks.

The first week brought four inspections with the agent, Janet, able to give the Smiths a few hours' notice. There were no offers and Janet reported that the buyers felt there were other properties that were better value for that price.

Week two - no ads and fairly quiet.

Week three - three enquiries from the ad with no offers.

Week four - nothing

Week five - before this ad went in they had another conference. Agnes, Jack, Joe and agent Janet.

At this conference it was decided to try a different advertising strategy that "just might work" according to Janet. She suggested that instead of using a price, they should advertise "suit buyers from $220,000". Agnes particularly was uncomfortable with this and needed persuading that maybe it would attract a buyer in the lower price range and then they could be encouraged to pay more. So with two (Jack and Joe) against one (Agnes) this strategy was employed for that ad!

Result – three enquiries and inspections with their first offer – $225,000! Agnes said "I told you so!" and Janet explained that they could make a counter offer of a higher price. They did this, changing the contract to $240,000. After much discussion the buyers decided that they couldn't go as high as that and decided to "keep looking".

Joe rang Janet and asked her to change the price for the property was advertised in the window to $240,000 (from the original $250,000). One more inspection and the weeks went by. By now it had been on the market for more than two months, and while Agnes and Jack had not originally been concerned with time, they were now getting tired of the indecision. Then the retirement village rang and said that a unit the size they wanted had become available. Joe contacted the village and negotiated the price of the unit so that his parents could afford to take a little less than first thought for their current home.

Janet was contacted. As chance happened the buyers who had put in the offer still hadn't bought. She advised them to make another offer, which they made at $230,000, and all were happy.

This was an amount that now allowed Agnes and Jack to do what they wanted to do.

What happened?

- At first time wasn't important so they were content to wait.
- There was little disruption to their daily routine.

- The limited advertisements and promotion meant fewer potential buyers.
- When the time factor became important they were satisfied with $230,000.

They started with privacy a top priority and speed of sale of little consequence:

1	**Privacy/least inconvenience and no publicity**
2	Best possible price
3	Shortest time

Eventually, due to changing circumstances, speed of sale moved to top requirement:

1	**Shortest time**
2	Privacy/least inconvenience and no publicity
3	Best possible price

Changed circumstances often result in changed priorities.

Case Study 6 - Norma and Roy Thomas

While the other case studies were based on what could happen in different circumstances, this case study relates to a situation I encountered. It is so typical of what can happen that I have related the story as it occurred, although I've changed the names (a little!) to protect the privacy of both sellers and purchasers (should they read this, both parties will recognise themselves, I'm sure!).

The owners – Roy and Norma – thought that maybe it was time to move. Their children had dispersed and they thought they'd consider a unit closer to the city. They lived in an area where houses didn't sell really quickly so they felt they had plenty of time to look around once their home was on the market.

This house was just three streets away from the home of buyers (Pam and David) who had been looking for a property with me for ages. They didn't have to sell their home before they bought and in fact absolutely loved their current home and wanted to stay in the area. But the house was too small and the land wasn't really big enough to allow or warrant an extension. Walking through Norma and Roy's house that had just been listed for sale was quite eerie, it was the same as Pam and David's (the buyers) house – exactly the same floor plan, a similar colour scheme, with an extra bedroom, bathroom and living area, and on a large block of land. Obviously, it had been built by the same builder – 30 years before! It was real goose-bumps stuff. Of course, the moment I got back to the office (pre mobile phone days!) I phoned Pam and told her I'd found a house for them and I'd pick them both up as soon as David got home from work. I also told them to "bring your cheque book". Like me, when they saw it they were most excited and overwhelmed with their good fortune. They offered the full price at which it was listed and a settlement of 30 days and insisted that I complete the contract then and there! By this time it was 7.00pm and never before or since have I filled out a contract on the bonnet of my car and lit by a streetlight!

They insisted on waiting in my car as they didn't anticipate a problem. Neither did I. The owners, however, were very concerned.

- "Should we have asked for more?"
- "Where will we live – we haven't found another house yet?"
- "Why would it sell so quickly?"
- "Did it sell this quickly because it was under priced?"

Case Study 6 - Norma and Roy Thomas

Every one of those questions was valid and this early offer had frightened them, even though I'd tried to warn them, without raising their hopes too high, when I'd seen the property that afternoon. I'd explained that I would like to bring a buyer through later that afternoon who could be interested. Such a dilemma! I felt for both parties. And all I could do was explain the situation and why this buyer offered full price – because they really wanted it. Probably the price was at the top end of what they could expect but it wasn't ridiculous. Would they have got more if they'd auctioned it? Who knows! I did believe that these buyers were the only people most likely to pay that price. After about an hour of talking, all the questions were resolved except "where will we move to"? I changed the settlement date to 90 days with the condition that the sellers could shorten that time at any stage with seven days' notice. This meant that they could find something else without having to panic. It made no difference to Pam and David, as they hadn't decided whether to sell or retain their current home for rental. Both parties initialled the changes and the deal was done.

While this was an extreme case, the first offer does sometimes come from a buyer with whom the agent has already been working. Of course, exactly the same thing can come from the first open home.

Asked to prioritise Roy and Norma probably would have said:

1	Best possible price
2	Privacy/least inconvenience and no publicity
3	Shortest time

We'd barely had time to discuss anything, but when their price ambition was realised, the speed of the sale was almost a hindrance! However, all's well that ends well!

Conclusion

So now we've come to the finality! This book has been written to give you more confidence with any problems that you may encounter when selling your home.

Obviously, I have my passions - what I would do if I was selling! - but I've been determined to remain objective.

I realise that everyone is different. I don't want people to have the wrong expectations from the course that they are undertaking. If they have confidence in their choice and know realistically what to expect, then I'll rest content! If one understands the journey that selling entails, then a lot of accompanying stress will be avoided.

It is my wish that you will be blessed with appointing an agent with whom you increasingly build confidence. Someone who has been a good listener, has defined your options, has accepted your choices, has communicated with you frequently and clearly, kept you honestly informed and has "been with you" all the way through.

I wish you success!

What Real Estate Agents Really Mean When They Say...

Agency - Real Estate Agency etc.

This is the actual office of the business that employs the real estate agents. Any agreement that you sign is with the agency via the agent. An agency must be under the control of a fully licensed real estate agent. To obtain what is called a "full" licence certain training and qualifications are required. This training involves real estate law, accounting, building laws etc and is usually spread over three to four years with a certain amount of time within the industry also being mandatory in nearly every case. There are a lot of variables in the above as the requirements are different in each area. Contrary to public opinion, a LOT of study is required to become a fully licensed agent who is able to own or manage an office as opposed to obtaining a real estate agent's sales licence.

Agent

Real Estate Agent, Real Estate Representative, or Real Estate "Rep" – again all mean the same.

An agent is an employee of the "agency". All real estate agents are "licensed salespeople" and have to complete certain training before obtaining that licence. The training differs from state to state and country to country.

Auction

This process has been analysed in this book but I felt that this was an appropriate time to tell some of the stories about the origins of the auction system. I cannot vouch for the veracity of these theories, as they're even older than I am!

Supposedly this system of selling started with the way in which Roman soldiers disposed of their spoils of war. They would gather all their loot and put a bloodstained shirt (evidently always one of those was available!) on a post to indicate that they were selling. That "shirt" nowadays is represented by the red auction flag. Then using "Auctio" (I increase) as their bid, the sale started. It's too long since I learnt Latin but I've been told that "auctio" did denote increase.

Then the auction system was also used in Babylon to dispose of slaves where even then they recognised that "black and white" is never right! Only the young, good-looking slaves were sold by auction and the older, less desirable slaves were sold by private negotiation! Now doesn't that tell you something? As I said I can't guarantee whether or not that's right but I've read and heard it from many different sources. It sounds feasible.

Campaign - as in "advertising campaign"

This refers to the period of time that the property is being advertised and promoted in order to get a sale. You may decide to have a "short" campaign with condensed promotion or a "long" campaign where you spread the advertising over a longer period – it's up to you.

Comparative Market Analysis

Real estate agents have access to data detailing sales of all property. Actually the public has the same access if they go to the relevant government department, pay a fee and stand in line! It is possible for agents to give you examples of past sales in your area. While these figures are not completely up to date they are more accurate than using current properties on the market. Make sure you're comparing "apples with apples" i.e. same size house, land area and suburb.

Controlled Listing

This is any form of selling where you commit to one agency to market/sell your property as opposed to giving it to lots of agents (open listing).

Conveyancing

All the legal work required to transfer a property from one owner to another. It's much more difficult than you think and involves a lot of tedious research, as well as the expertise of trained solicitors/conveyancers to recognise problems.

Days on market

The length of time it takes your property to sell – from the day of signing the selling agreement to the day of signing the contract. This is handy information to help you decide which method of selling you'll choose. Of course, all that can be given is the "average", but some methods of selling have, on average, fewer days of selling than other methods.

Investor

I've used this term to denote the person who has bought or owns a property (or properties) purely for the purpose of renting it out and using it as an investment. In essence we are all investors, as the home you live in is most certainly an important investment.

List

A real estate term that denotes the giving of "the rights to sell" your property to an agent/agents. Guess it comes from the fact that it goes on their "list" of houses to sell. Can't think of any other derivative for that term.

Market feedback

This is a dreadful real estate term that I think always sounds as if the market has indigestion! It's the term used when letting the owners know what potential buyers and people "in the market" think or say about their property. Certainly, accurate market information is the best indication of the value of your property.

Open Homes - Open for Inspections - Home Opens

All of these terms mean the same and are practically self-explanatory. Your home is "opened to the public". All agents will take the name and phone numbers of all attendees as a courtesy to the owner and also as a security precaution. If you don't intend "robbing" the house, then what's the harm in giving your name? Any attendee is at liberty to ask the agent NOT to call them. Privacy laws preclude those names to be used for any other purpose unless it's specifically requested and permission is given by the attendee.

Owner/Builder

A very courageous (or experienced!) person who employs sub-contractors to build his/her/their house. The owner-builder organises the permits, usually purchases the material and then employs each sub-contractor. Some areas have legislation where, if a property has been "owner-built", the fact must be declared to the prospective purchaser - not ALL areas have that by-law, just some.

Qualifying

This is a term used to denote the process of talking to buyers in order to find out what they are likely to buy and how much they are likely to pay. Sometimes agents ask so many questions that they form a very "black and white" picture of what they believe the buyers will buy. Guess what? They're often wrong! Some questions are essential, especially regarding their finances, but an agent can "over-qualify" a buyer, form an incorrect opinion and decide not to show them a property that otherwise they may buy. The answer is, "qualify" but beware of agents who "over-qualify".

Reserve

This is a figure below which an auctioneer cannot, without your permission, sell your property at auction – i.e. "under the hammer" (see "Under the Hammer"). The reserve is usually decided on, between several days and several hours before the auction. By this time you have a good idea of what potential buyers are saying and if you DO want to sell, those figures will be your guide in setting the reserve. You may decide that if you cannot get a certain amount, you won't sell. Either your salesperson or the auctioneer will discuss the "reserve" with you, but at this point, remember IT IS YOUR CHOICE! The reserve is written on to the auction agreement and initialled by all selling parties at this time.

Sometimes an owner will say: "This is my reserve (for example, $350,000), but if it gets to $330,000 come and talk to me." At that stage it will depend on whether there is more than one bidder etc. That's when the auctioneer stops the auction to talk to you or asks the salesperson "to seek further instructions!" Usually then the auctioneer or salesperson will talk to you to advise what is happening. You may at this time decide to change the reserve (down not up!) You should initial this change where indicated to avoid any misunderstanding.

Once the reserve has been reached the auctioneer can then sell the property without further consultation. You can't change your mind! An auctioneer CANNOT sell a property below the reserve without express permission from you.

Settlement

The date on which the money is paid to the owner's solicitors and the purchased property legally belongs to the new buyer. Settlement is usually effected between solicitors/conveyancers. Banks are involved if mortgages need to be discharged. You cannot take possession of the property before it has "settled" unless, with specific legal instructions and conditions, and you must have completely vacated the property by that date. Often the buyer (always accompanied by the agent) wishes to have a "final inspection" on the morning the property will be settled. This is not to decide whether or not they still want to buy it (it's too late for THAT!) but to check on inclusions and to make sure that the property hasn't been changed between the sale and settlement. The settlement date is stated on the contract and is either stated as an actual date or as the number of days from the date of the contract. Should that date be a weekend or holiday, settlement takes place on the NEXT working day. Agents should, however, always check to see that this is not the case.

The time between signing and settlement can vary. Anything under seven days is VERY difficult and should be avoided unless under exceptional circumstances (example in "Auctions are flexible!") Under normal circumstances the time will vary between 30 and 90 days - but remember, you can change to suit your circumstances.

Under bidder

The disappointed person who missed out. Someone obviously bid higher and for whatever reason – probably not enough money – this bidder was unsuccessful.

"Under-the-Hammer"

That's when auctions are such fun for everyone – auctioneer, salespersons and especially for you, the owner. A sale "under-the-hammer" is one where the reserve has been reached or exceeded, all bidding has been exhausted and the auctioneer brings his gavel (hammer in ancient days) down (after LOTS of warning and exhortation to the bidders to keep going!) and the sale is made. A sale "under-the-hammer" has no extra conditions and is a cash sale with 10% deposit payable immediately. You, the owner, is the person who nominates conditions on an auction contract.